Notes on a Past Life

Also by David Trinidad

Pavane (1981)
Monday, Monday (1985)
Living Doll (1986)
November (1987)
Three Stories (1988)
Hand Over Heart: Poems 1981-1988 (1991)
Answer Song (1994)
Essay with Movable Parts (1998)
Plasticville (2000)
Tiny Moon Notebook (2007)
The Late Show (2007)
Dear Prudence: New and Selected Poems (2011)
Peyton Place: A Haiku Soap Opera (2013)

Collaborations

A Taste of Honey (with Bob Flanagan, 1990)
Chain Chain Chain (with Jeffery Conway and
    Lynn Crosbie, 2000)
Phoebe 2002: An Essay in Verse (with Jeffery
    Conway and Lynn Crosbie, 2003)
By Myself: An Autobiography (with D.A. Powell,
    2009)

Editor

Powerless: Selected Poems 1973-1990
    by Tim Dlugos (1996)
*Holding Our Own: The Selected Poems of Ann
    Stanford* (with Maxine Scates, 2001)
*Saints of Hysteria: A Half-Century of Collaborative
    American Poetry* (with Denise Duhamel and
    Maureen Seaton, 2007)
A Fast Life: The Collected Poems of Tim Dlugos (2011)

Notes on a Past Life

poems by

David Trinidad

BLAZEVOX[BOOKS]
Buffalo, New York

publisher of weird little books

BlazeVOX [books]

blazevox.org

BlazeVOX

To Jimmy

Let it be felt that the painter was there, seeing things in their own light.

—Pierre Bonnard

Contents

I. Lost Illusions

It's 1990 and I'm still new 17
Jimmy's Moon 20
Five from the Archive 22
Lost Illusions 25
"a few pink minutes" 34
Allen was not the best teacher 37
At the End of the Dream I Can Fly 43

II. Someday I'll Live and Make Art Here

c/o Peter Drake 47
Commonplace 62
Elaine 65
Joe 73
Acker is back in New York 77
Tim 82
From a Notebook 87
I called Eileen 88

III. Three Tall Women

Anaïs 95
Ann Stanford stood at the blackboard 101
I met May Swenson just once, ... 111

IV. Poets

After Ashbery 117
To Adrienne Rich 119
No More Blurbs 122
Poets 123

Susan takes me to the Academy of American Poets 128
Commonplace 131

V. Man with Toy

The radiator is clanking... 137
My Yoko Ono Moment 143
For Jeffery, ... 145
A Few Words About My Collecting................................. 152
What was I doing in Lawrence, Kansas, ... 157
From a Notebook... 163
The Breakup Poem 164
Man with Toy 168

VI. 9/11

9/11 173

VII. Two Odes

Ode to Frank O'Hara 185
At Sexton's Grave.. 189

VIII. Leaving New York

Leaving New York.. 199
Byron wants his belly rubbed... 207
Almost twenty years later, Eileen and I met 217
After Ginsberg.. 221
Snow on the ground outside... 230

Notes on a Past Life

I

Lost Illusions

nothing is really ever forgotten,
merely filed away
                    —Edward Albee

It's 1990 and I'm still new

to New York: I don't understand
what winter is. Snow is so
strange: freshly fallen, it's cold and
not cold at the same time. And so quiet.
I crunch through it, hair wet
from the shower, no hat,
green thrift-shop tweed coat,
to my part-time job at the Chelsea Hotel.
In New York poets are slaves of
the Art World, so I work as
assistant to Inanout Press,
a chaotic affair run by two
women Raymond introduced me to—
Paola Igliori and Michele Zalopany.
Their first effort, painted poems
by Rene Ricard, caused a
recent stir downtown.
A dark, narrow hallway
opens to Michele's spacious room:
nothing but an antique table and chair,
sleigh bed, and long thin curtains
that billow cold air from the balcony—
a balustrade just like Jimmy's.
He's in his much smaller room
downstairs, right this minute,
writing his wonderful poems.
Last week we saw *After Dark, My Sweet*,
afterwards ate where we always eat:
his favorite Chinese on 23rd Street.
I admire Michele's paintings:
literal and detailed, they
have a misty sheen, the grainy beauty

of black-and-white films.
And I like her: cropped
bleached-blonde hair, full
body and face, she's as compelling
as Simone Signoret in her
middle age. She has a little
dog named Louie I sometimes walk
around the block. I smoke
as I type, at the table, while
Paola and Michele sit cross-legged
on the bed, planning, chaotically,
their next project: a collection of rap
lyrics (rumor has it that Michele likes
black men). The book is never
to be. In the bathroom, on the clear
shower curtain: a map of the world—
funny what one remembers. Paola
is slender and sharp-edged, high
strung, with a mass of wild
curly brown hair. Known as
the Hazelnut Heiress—the nuts
in Baci chocolates, the ones wrapped
in silver foil with blue stars, at
cash registers at all of the greengrocers,
come from her family's orchards
in Italy, or so I've heard—
she lives in a sparsely furnished
brownstone on the Lower East Side
with her son (from her marriage
to artist Sandro Chia) and Paul,
Raymond's young assistant, whom
she's recently taken up with (much
to Raymond's displeasure). Paola
owns buttons that once belonged to
Marie Antoinette, mentions them often.

After Michele moves to Italy,
to paint for a while, I work with
Paola downtown, but, without
Michele's groundedness, find her too
scattered and contradictory to be around.
I start seeing a therapist (he falls
asleep during one of our sessions)
to help me deal with her. When it
dawns on me I'm paying the therapist
as much as I make working for Paola,
I quit both. Later I hear, probably
from Raymond, that Paola has accused
Paul of molesting her son, and run
into her every so often at art openings—
manic, boundaryless, a must to avoid.
Paola who, whenever she needed
an influx of funds, sold some
of Marie Antoinette's buttons.
Who fed me broccoli rabe (I'd
never had it before) on white winter
mornings. Who made a delicious
carrot soup. Who said charming
things like: "I have an absolute *thirst*
for olive oil." Funny what one remembers.

Jimmy's Moon

It wasn't until
Jimmy died
that I realized
the first poem
of his I ever read
was the little one
about seeing the
crescent moon through
the window of
a train, "En Route
to Southampton,"
which my friend
Rachel had clipped
from *The New Yorker*
and pinned to
the bulletin board
in her kitchen
a matter of months
before the accident.
The poem didn't
do much for me,
as I stood there
and read it,
having no idea,
of course, that
Rachel would soon
die and I survive
and come to love
Schuyler's work
and be his friend.
A kind of prediction,
or icy promise,

like Jimmy's moon,
a dead friend's
introduction to
a future friend,
who, as it turned
out, was now dead
too. Rachel liked
short poems.

Five from the Archive

4:11 a.m.

Just in time to see
Carol Lynley get
eaten by the Blob
in *Beware! the Blob*.

*

October 22, 1988

It's cold, wet
and windy in
NYC. Sharon,
Carl and I take
the 2 train up-
town to hear
Eileen and Paul
read. Joan will
be there. Elaine
is at work. Dennis
has a deadline.
Jerome has a cold.

*

Subway

Below:
vomit
& piss

Above:
whiff of
fresh
donuts

*

What Debbie & Cameron Lost in New York

Cameron's Walkman

Debbie's glasses

All of Cameron's demo tapes

Debbie's lipstick

Debbie's earrings

2 hats (his & hers)

Their return tickets

Approximately 100 bucks

*

At an Opening

You look—Great!

Isn't this a beautiful show?

It is now.

(Silence)

I didn't say that.

Lost Illusions

*"My poor boy, like you I came here with my heart full of
illusions, spurred on by the love of art, swept forwards by
an invincible yearning for fame."* —Balzac

In Manhattan everything's happening
too fast: readings, openings, parties.
Wherever Tim Dlugos goes, I follow—
dazzled, never quite able to catch my breath.
Tonight it's to this and that
event, then to Ann Lauterbach's
loft in Tribeca. "But Tim," I fret
as we exit the cab, "we weren't *invited*."
No use: he bounds up
the stairs ahead of me.
Jimmy's there (a fleeting hello,
but I'll see him next week
for a movie and Chinese),
and Elaine and Jerome (as new
to all this as I am), and Joe
and Kenward and Ron
and countless others. John
Ashbery, whom Tim charges through
the crowd to chat up.
Barbara Guest, whom I kneel down
to introduce myself to.
John Ash (whom Tim detests),
who is so plastered
he falls out of his chair
onto the floor, spilling his drink
on himself. Unfazed, he keeps
talking, cigarette hand
waving in my direction.
I am five years sober, and polite.

Another night, Dennis and I
go to hear Eileen read at a bar
on the Lower East Side.
I idolize Eileen, spend as
much time with her as I can.
She's unkempt (in a cool way),
butch (dresses like a boy),
swaggeringly charismatic.
Mesmerized by her Boston accent,
I've accompanied her
to her walk-up on Third Street
(across from the Hells Angels
clubhouse). Bathtub in kitchen.
Through rusty cross-hatched
window gates: fire escapes,
bare trees, cemetery statues
draped in snow. (I know this view
from her poems.) No door
on the bathroom; exposed, I try
to pee soundlessly. Eileen
made sure that Anne Waldman
included me in *Out of This World:
An Anthology of the St. Mark's
Poetry Project 1966-1991*.
I'm featuring Eileen in the issue
of *Brooklyn Review* I'm co-editing.
(The cover will be a vivid red.)
I haven't missed any of her readings
since I moved to New York.
She seems to give voice to everything
that's bottled up inside me.
She has guts and street smarts,
and lives, fully, the life
of the writer, which after
working for the Housing Authority

in Los Angeles for seven years,
I long to do. We've been
long-distance friends for six
of those seven years: given
readings together, written
letters (I love her scrawly handwriting),
had long late-night conversations
on the phone, even put each other up.
Early on, we drank together;
then Eileen joined the fellowship,
inspired me to do the same.
I sensed sometimes that my
"conversion," my exuberant
talk about having a spiritual awakening,
got on her nerves. When
Jimmy "flipped" over my chapbook
Monday, Monday, Tim told me Eileen
had referred to me as an "Eve."
I called her; she denied saying it.
But admitted to finding,
on Jimmy's desk (she worked
as his assistant), a letter
recommending me for a Whiting Award.
Why hadn't he recommended her?
I assured her I wasn't trying
to take anything away from her,
that I simply aspired to be her peer.
I thought that had soothed
her suspicion. Now that I'm
here in New York, hanging out with her
in person, I can tell things
aren't quite right between us.
She looks at me warily, head cocked
back and eyes squinted, acts
as if I'm trespassing on her turf.

Dennis and I stand in the bar and smoke,
wait for the reading to begin.
He wears a red Adidas T-shirt,
threadbare jeans and sneakers
(his youth costume), surveys the
turnout with a mixture of
excitement and disdain. Eileen
brings Marilyn Hacker (a lesbian
award-winner) over to introduce her
to him. Hacker proceeds to gush—
gesturing animatedly—
about how much she admires his work.
When Dennis casually says
(out of politeness? hoping to deflect?)
"This is David Trinidad,"
Hacker (Jimmy calls her
"the gay sonneteer") turns
to stone as she turns toward me.
"Nice to meet you," I muster.
She doesn't say a word, eyes huge
behind homely spectacles,
glaring at me with utter disregard.
She turns back to Dennis and
continues praising him.
No one I've met in New York
has made me feel so unimportant.

Until: a party at Darragh Park's
brownstone in Chelsea, after
an Ashbery reading. Dimly lit. Drinks.
A wheel of Brie, water crackers,
green and red grapes. A piano in
the shadows. Poets mingling, silhouetted
against the street light in the front
windows. (I'd noticed daffodils

in the flower boxes outside.)
Some of Darragh's paintings.
On one wall, spotlit, a cluster of
poems, each framed, dedicated
to our host. Like trophies. I study
them to see who they're by: Jimmy,
Tim, Marc Cohen, Tom. Will I
get to know Darragh well enough
to write a poem for him, end
up on his wall? I read
a few lines of the one by Douglas
Crase, and lo and behold:
standing in front of me, the real
Douglas Crase, thin and handsome,
flirting in that flattering and
harmless way of his. (People
say he's unable to write since
winning a MacArthur "genius"
award.) I squeeze a lime slice
into my Perrier and stick close to
Raymond: he has a comforting air
of self-confidence. I marvel
that I'm here, among the literati—
the New York School poets—
that I so admire. And lo and
behold: Ashbery himself is
standing in front of me. He
asks, in that nasal whine, that
brings to mind Truman Capote
drunk on a talk show, what I
thought of the poems he sent.
At Jimmy's insistence, I'd
solicited him for *Brooklyn Review*.
He'd sent two short poems
that didn't do much for us;

they felt like throwaways.
We'd agonized: How can we
reject John Ashbery? And
rationalized: His name will be
good for the magazine. Besides, I
don't want to displease Jimmy.
"I liked them," I answer, my
lack of enthusiasm obvious
put on the spot like that. "No
one's ever going to see your
little magazine," he snaps,
suddenly vicious. Then: "I
haven't liked anything you've
written since your first book."
As he swaggers off, Raymond
leans over: "Do you realize
what he just said?" Several others
stand within hearing distance.
(Memory has blacked out their faces.)
Will they spread word of this
insult around? Will people think
less of me? The next time I visit
Jimmy at the Chelsea, I tell
him what John said. He looks
surprised. Then, after a long
pause: "Well, John was drunk."

Tension has been building between
Eileen and me. When she calls
to make a coffee date, I'm so swamped
I can't meet till the following week.
A few days later, Jeffery calls:
"Did you put off getting together
with Eileen?" "Yes. How did
you know?" He heard her share

at a meeting in the East Village:
Who does he think he is? Jeffery
could tell she was talking about me.
"So much for anonymity."
When Ira and I start dating,
she calls him at Grove Press
(where he's publicity director):
What can you do for my career?
Her aggressiveness works his nerves;
he has no patience for her after that.
1988, 1989: I'm invited to
Jimmy's annual birthday dinner
at Chelsea Central, a swank
steak house on 10th Avenue.
A "men only" affair—Joe,
John, Darragh, Raymond—
all in dress shirts and blazers.
I follow suit and order my fillet
medium rare, savor the potatoes
au gratin, the lemon sorbet,
but don't say very much.
Intimidated to be in such stellar
company, I stare at the breadcrumbs
on the white tablecloth, at
the red rose in the bud vase.
No "Happy Birthday to You":
Jimmy doesn't like to be sung to.
Eileen's agitated that
I've been admitted into the
"inner circle"—and that it's all male.
I'm careful not to lord it over her
even though she's invited to plenty
of things that I'm not, like the dinner
after Jimmy's spectacular Dia reading.
When I have poems in *Under 35*:

*The New Generation of American
Poets*, she says, "I should've been
in that." Why can't I say, "Eileen,
you're thirty-nine years old"?
She can barely contain her fury
when Ira and Amy Scholder
fail to include her in *High Risk:
An Anthology of Forbidden Writings*.
She expects me to persuade Ira
to put her in it. "I've told him
he should, Eileen. What more
can I do?" "He's *your* boyfriend!"
I don't dare tell her it's because
he dislikes her. They share the
same birthday: December ninth.
I feel the brunt of this coincidence.

A party (one of the first of the fall)
at Doug and Frank's apartment—
so many books, obscured by
chattering poets. Biding my
time in the kitchen while Eileen
networks in the living room,
waiting till she's ready to leave.
Why didn't I just go? Why *not*
give Marjorie Welish the opportunity
to slight me? (Charles North:
"Marjorie, this is David Trinidad.
He's written haiku about '60s TV shows."
Marjorie: "We never had a *television*
in our home.") Afterwards, standing
with Eileen on a dark corner in Chelsea,
on the west side of Ninth Avenue: *I cried.
All my friends are in that book.* I see
(dimly) that she's never going to

get past this *High Risk* business.
"I'm sorry. I wish we could both be in it."
1990: a late-night phone call
(one of our last). I've recently
moved in with Ira; he's asleep
in the back of the loft. This year,
Eileen informs me, she's finally
attending Jimmy's birthday dinner
at Chelsea Central. Pause.
"Tomorrow night." Stunned
that I wasn't invited, I express
my surprise out loud: "Does
this mean I've fallen out of
Jimmy's favor?" Silence.
Eileen waits long enough to
let her triumph sink in, and
to savor my hurt. Then she
says, "I'm going to hang up."
And hangs up.

"a few pink minutes"

I'd come out of the subway
at Seventh Avenue and walk
west on 23rd Street
until I reached the red brick
and black balustrade facade
of the Hotel Chelsea,
enter through the glass doors,
and wait in the lobby
(I was always early), smoke
a cigarette (or two) and soak
up the seedy glamour:
every inch of wall space covered
with the atrocious art of previous
tenants, an elderly lady taking
her equally elderly terrier
for a walk, and young rockers
ten years too late for punk,
ragged sleeveless denim
flaunting pale skeletal arms.
When it was time, I'd ride an
elevator (there were two to
choose from, one on either side
of the front desk) to the sixth floor.
Once, a blonde girl stood
at the end of the white hall,
watching me. A ghost?
She could have been. Otherwise,
it was usually empty, hushed.
I'd knock on the door—
625—and he'd welcome me
into his one-room world:
single bed with mussed-up

sheets (I don't think
I ever saw it made), television,
desk, a leaning tower of LPs—
handsome Brook Benton on top—
and books—shelves of them, but
I only remember *The Portrait
of a Lady* (I was reading it
for a lit class) and Elizabeth
Bishop's *North & South* (which
I handled like the Holy Grail).
A dull yellow file cabinet
(two-drawer), locked (he kept
cash and unfinished poems in it).
A low bedside table, lamp,
push-button phone. Lots
of pill bottles and clutter.
White shuttered doors slid
closed on the kitchenette.
On the walls, art from the
covers of *The Crystal Lithium*
and *A Few Days*: Fairfield
Porter's watercolor (frothing
purple waves), Darragh's
painting (verdure rife
with pink and lavender).
The Porter, as I recall, was
beginning to slip out of its
frame. In the bathroom, a
green bottle: Ajaccio Violets
(the cologne he splashes
on himself in the poem he
gave me for *Brooklyn Review*).
By the door, stacks of
mysteries—he had a soft
spot for Elmore Leonard—

spines heavily creased.
Bouts of insomnia? Those
stacks would grow a bit taller
between visits. Barbara,
the cat he adopted when
Tom left for the friary in
San Francisco, was curled
somewhere. I don't remember
ever petting her, or her coming
to me. Aloof? Depressed?
After one visit, I wrote a sketch
of his room; if I hadn't, certain
details would be lost to me.
An oak leaf taped to a mirror.
An orange and white scarf
laid over the typewriter.
Three small apples on the TV.
A can of Diet Pepsi. Yellow
and salmon carnations in
a blue bottle on the file cabinet.
At the end of another visit,
I fetched him a BLT from the
greasy spoon on the corner
of Eighth Avenue. At the end
of another, before heading
back to Brooklyn, I sat in
an armchair near the French
doors and watched, through
the wrought-iron flowers
of the balustrade, a sunset
that was pure Freilicher—
sky a haze of blue-gray
above smokestacks and
shadowy brick—transfixed
for a few pink minutes.

Allen was not the best teacher

on the planet: he was narcissistic
(only liked poems that mimicked his own)
and insensitive (he once needled Mary Greene,
my co-editor on *Brooklyn Review*, until she
burst into tears and rushed out of the room;
it was difficult to respect him after that)
and made us meditate, with our eyes open,
at the beginning of each class (which seemed
silly to me). But it always felt special to be
in his presence. There I was, sitting next to
this famous poet, the author of *Kaddish* and
Howl, a Beat icon. Some people assumed
that I'd come to Brooklyn College specifically
to study with him. If I had, I'd have been
doubly disappointed: he didn't understand
what I was up to. "Where's the epiphany, Trinidad?"
he asked more than once. It would have been
too easy to suggest that perhaps I didn't intend
there to be an epiphany, so I kept quiet. His
monomania irritated me. I was older than
the other students (thirty-five) and had already
published several books. My poems, of late, were
stiff and labored—a struggle to pull words
out of me. I'd hoped my move to New York
would shock me from this stasis, and that going
back to school would help loosen me up.
Who else was in that workshop? Languagey
Karen Kelley (years later Clayton Eshleman,
who published her in *Sulfur*, told me she had
worked as a stripper), painfully shy Paul Beatty
(he would go on to become a novelist), darkly
earnest Peter Money (under the Beat spell

but likable). One week, Gregory Corso filled
in for Allen, off being Ginsberg somewhere
on the globe, and spent the whole time trying
to hit on Pamela Hughes, the prettiest girl
in the room. When a classmate and I whispered
to each other, Corso snapped, "What are
you guys, CIA?" (The following year, at the big
Hanuman Books reading at St. Mark's Church,
as my Barbie poem went over well with the crowd,
Corso said to Raymond, "This guy really knows
his stuff.") Students complained about Corso,
which miffed Allen. The next time, Alice Notley
subbed: I could have listened to her talk about
poetry forever. She read Olson's "The Librarian"
and instructed us to remember a dream and
write a poem about it. "I never remember my
dreams," I whined. "You will." Alice was right,
I did remember one, but the poem that resulted,
about not being able to recall the title of a book
of poems Madonna had published, was a dud.
I wrote it in my notebook as I sat with Sharon
Mesmer in the Campus Cafe across from
the college. Sharon, whom I'd met in Chicago
when I read there a few years before, entered
the MFA program the same time as me. Fate
(in the form of the English Department) set us up
as roommates: while one of the professors,
Nancy Black, was on a semester-long sabbatical,
we sublet her three-story brownstone on
Lincoln Road. Unbeknownst to me, Sharon
(blonde, aggressive, lean) moved in her
Chicago boyfriend Carl, a writer, whose face
was so pockmarked it was painful to look at him.
When not hunched over his green-screened IBM
computer, he catered to Sharon's every whim.

We shared the first floor (dining room and
kitchen), Sharon and Carl took the second,
and I the third: large front room adjoined by
a narrow, book-lined office; bathroom halfway
down the hall; and small room in the back,
which (except when Debbie and Cameron
slept there one chaotic weekend) I essentially
used as a closet. I spent most of my time
in the front room. It had everything I needed:
bed, desk, TV. I read *The Portrait of a Lady*
in that room: *What cared Isabel Archer for the
vulgar judgements of obscure people?* I listened
to Smiths cassettes on my yellow Walkman.
Wrote flirtatious letters to Jeffery in California
(he'd enroll at Brooklyn the following fall).
And inspired by Ted Berrigan's book of
postcard poems, *A Certain Slant of Sunlight*
(my first purchase at St. Mark's Bookshop),
which engendered, noted Alice, "a newly
freed voice," wrote a lot of short poems of
my own. There were pots of red geraniums
in a window across the street. I put them
in a slim lyric that Jimmy liked; he published it
in *Broadway 2: A Poets and Painters Anthology*.
One morning at 4:11, unable to sleep, I switched
on the TV in time to see Carol Lynley get
swallowed by the Blob in *Beware! The Blob*.
Dukakis lost to Bush in November. To cheer
ourselves up, my roommates and I decided
to host a Thanksgiving feast. They asked a few
of their friends; I invited Dennis, Elaine and
Jerome. After dessert, I took my guests
upstairs to watch *Mary Poppins*. The next
morning, I came down and made tea, then
started back up. Sharon was waiting for me

on the staircase, in a fury. *How rude of us
to have gotten up and left the table. Her friends
commented on it. Even they'd heard of Dennis—
they knew he was famous. How humiliating.
And they had to clean up after us. We just left
our dirty dishes. So rude and inconsiderate.
So selfish. Nasty. To be snubbed in front of her
friends. On Thanksgiving. By someone famous.*
Throughout Sharon's tirade, Carl hovered
protectively, two or three steps above her.
I had been inconsiderate, I realized. Faced with
her anger, I stubbornly withheld an apology.
No one had screamed at me like that since my
childhood—no, since my drunken twenties.
She stormed into her quarters, Carl in tow,
and slammed their door. I spilled tea as I made
my way to mine, where I sat for a while, shaking.
Sharon refused to speak to me for days. During
my next tutorial with Allen, I told him I was
having trouble with her. "Noblesse oblige,"
was his only response. I had to ask someone
else what that meant. Our sublet was up
in a matter of weeks; I steered clear of
Sharon as much as possible. I searched for,
and found, a one-year sublet on the Lower
East Side. I've tried to be truthful, over
the years, when students have asked what
Allen was like as a teacher. I've come to say,
"He was a mixed bag." I'm up front about
his faults, then tell them I also have some
touching memories. One night that first
September, Raymond and I met Ginsberg
and John Wieners at Odessa, a Ukrainian
restaurant facing Tompkins Square Park.
Allen looked up from their booth and said,

sweetly, "Hello, student." We shared an
order of cheese blintzes. Returning from
Christmas break, Allen announced, like a
giddy kid, that he'd spent New Year's Eve
with Madonna and Warren Beatty. I wasn't
impressed: one can be too in love with fame.
A couple of times, after long days at school,
Allen offered me a ride home (I'd moved
to Manhattan by then). A car service drove
him to and from Brooklyn College; I thought
that was the height of glamour. On one of
those rides, I asked him how he felt about
"Howl" being recited by Pia Zadora in a
John Waters movie. "They paid me one
hundred dollars," he said proudly. Ira and
I ran into him in Paris (I'd graduated by
then); he gave us a ride—a driver in every
city!—to a party honoring American artists.
At that soirée, I tried to explain to Philip Glass
why *Rosemary's Baby* was worth republishing
(in Ira's Midnight Classics series). Allen
was kind to me when my mother died. I
told him that "Kaddish" was the only poem
I could find about a son mourning his mother,
that it was helping me come to terms with my grief;
he wrote back suggesting I read Creeley's
"For My Mother." I had it in my bookcase
and didn't know it. It gave me great comfort.
And at the big reading at St. Mark's for the
Norton anthology of postmodern poetry,
Allen pronounced, at the podium, that there
were a number of interesting younger poets
in the book—"Dennis Cooper, Amy Gerstler,
David Trinidad." It smarted when, twenty
years later, I was cut from the second edition,

and Mesmer added. In the nineties, she'd been
associated with a group of poets that called
themselves The Unbearables (no comment).
After that fizzled out, she became involved
in Flarf, a fad started by, by all reports, a
bunch of attention-starved, self-proclaimed
avant-gardists. I took solace in the fact that
Schuyler and Berrigan were once dropped
from the second edition of a Norton. Then,
as Sharon's hate-filled face surfaced from the
depths like a remembered dream, I thought:
Noblesse oblige. Then: *Allen! You taught me that.*

At the End of the Dream I Can Fly

A woman   in a black kimono   dyed black hair
disappeared   behind a black curtain
I'd decided to give a poetry reading   in drag
A feather boa   many shades of blue
turned into   a string of seashells
Odd light   from elaborate lampshades
antique furniture   Sally Kellerman's
I couldn't find the right   high-heels
so decided   not to do the reading in drag
I might not be able to   handle it

Outside   my automobile   a small red truck
wasn't where   I parked it   Carloads of men
all in the same   red gown and blonde wig
began arriving   for the reading   A guy
I think he was flirting   sang   to me
but then he   put his arm around   another guy
I had to find my truck   I took a shortcut
through a fenced courtyard   A long line
of schoolgirls wearing party dresses carrying balloons
marched towards me   I jumped up   to avoid them

On the next street   a wild dog   chasing me
teeth   viciously snapping at   my feet
As I ran   along a path   that twisted
through some trees   I realized I was flying
flying   high enough   to escape the dog
and could see   all the backyards   below
like the neighborhood   where I grew up
and I thought   *my red truck   my red truck*

3/7/89

II

Someday I'll Live
and Make Art Here

c/o Peter Drake

I've decided being
new in New York
is a permanent frame
of mind. It's been
a year already &
I still don't feel
comfortable here.
Everything's moving
too fast—a slash of
green, then yellow
paint; a gray, rain-
slick blur. Horns
honk, the subway
rumbles underfoot.
The crowd pushes
past a homeless soul
in a soiled sleeping
bag in the middle
of the sidewalk. A
bald man in a hos-
pital gown stands
on the corner of the
next block, scream-
ing. I just want to sit
somewhere & smoke
a cigarette & think.

Everyone says it takes
at least two years . . .

Will I ever get used
to winter? I don't like
how hats mess up
my hair, can't stand
cold air on my neck.
Joan says the secret
to keeping warm is
to wear layers. Paul
advises me to mois-
turize. (Because his
face is heavily lined?)

Tim sends me a Christ-
mas card (with angels).

When I graduate, will
I move back to L.A.?

A fifth-floor walk-up at 249 East Second Street
where Houston & Second, running parallel,
come to a point at Avenue C,
sublet (illegally) from artist Peter Drake
while he's on a yearlong residency in Germany.
A tiny closet of an apartment, all white,
with two windows that face a defunct theater
turned (illegal) nightclub called The World.
Through a hole in the floor near the radiator,
I hear the man in the apartment below
abuse his girlfriend. (Peter warned
me about this.) Next door there's a gas station;
on the corner, a "bodega" (a New York word)
where I buy yogurt & muffins & Marlboro Lights.
Every month I mail a money order to the landlord
as if I were Peter Drake.

Hedda Nussbaum's battered face &
Marla Hanson's slashed face &
the assault & rape of the Central Park jogger
are all over the tabloids.

The pulsating beat of the disco across the street
makes it difficult to study or sleep.
I wear earplugs as I read the Romantics one semester,
the Victorians the next. "Where shall I learn to get
my peace again?" I underline (in pencil) in Keats.
In Arnold: "this strange disease of modern life ..."
Shelley's "To a Skylark" is a favorite: "Our sweetest
songs are those that tell of saddest thought."
As is Coleridge's "Frost at Midnight."
I write papers on Byron's "Darkness" & Tennyson's
   Maud
& fall in love with Dorothy Wordsworth's journals
(which Jimmy, fellow diary-lover, is happy to hear):
"God be thanked I want not society by a moonlight
   lake."

    What I moved to
    New York with:
    one suitcase stuffed
    full of clothes &
    one box of books.
    Now I own at least
    twice as many books
    (can't stop buying
    them), a clock radio,
    an off-white touch-
    tone phone, an elec-
    tric typewriter (with
    correction tape) &

a Mr. Coffee (which
gurgles & hisses as
I impatiently wait
each morning: can't
light my first ciga-
rette without a sip
of that awful stuff,
sweetened to accept-
ability with half a
pink packet of sac-
charin). There's
a loft reached by a
steep ladder above
a built-in desk that
I refuse to use: too
high up (close to
ceiling) & no railing
I'm afraid I'll roll
over & fall out while
I sleep. On Orchard
Street, I buy a convert-
ible futon sofa bed—
my biggest purchase
to date; pay to have
it delivered, but don't
know enough to tip
the men who haul it
up four flights of stairs.
Though I follow the
assembly instructions
to a tee, the middle
keeps collapsing when
the futon's folded out.
Ronna, a classmate
at Brooklyn College

who has power tools,
comes over & drills
screws into the wood
frame: the now perma-
nently open bed takes
up most of the apart-
ment. I do everything
on it: sleep, eat, mas-
turbate, read, write.

I tape a black-&-
white photograph
of Anne Sexton—
long legs crossed
around each other,
holding her ubiq-
uitous cigarette—
torn from a poetry
anthology, to the
wall above the bed.

In storage in my
parents' garage in
Central California:
ten boxes of books
& two bankers boxes
of poems & corre-
spondence. Most
precious: three years
of letters from Jimmy:
"Thank you for writ-
ing the poems you
do. I feel sincerely
privileged to read
them." My friend

Christopher in Los
Angeles is looking
after my art. Most
treasured: my Jim
Isermann starburst
clock, painted red
& yellow & blue, o-
riginally part of his
1983 *Look Forward to
Tomorrow* installation.
Second most prized:
Password, a painting
by Mark Kroening
from his "Espionage
& Intrigue" series
(two spies in silhou-
ette against a slate
blue background, one
of them lighting the
other's cigarette with
a yellow-red flame)
in custom-made Iser-
mann frame: wavy
corrugated wood
trim (painted red).

Dennis & Eileen & I get out of a taxi in front of
The Kitchen, a performance space on 19th Street
between 10th Avenue & the Chelsea Piers.
We've come to hear two poets from L.A.: Michael
    Lassell
& La Loca (real name Pamala Karol). I met Michael,
a corpulent gay poet who has been
getting a lot of attention for his AIDS poem
"How to Watch Your Brother Die," just before I

left Los Angeles. He took me to see
Gavin Dillard, a.k.a. "The Naked Poet," of whom he
is enamored, give a reading. Dillard (long-haired,
hard-bodied, teen-idol cute), who appears
in gay porn films as Gavin Jeffrey, peeled off
all his clothes & recited his poems
next to an ornate brass candelabra
with eight lit white candles.

La Loca's *Adventures on the Isle of Adolescence* is
the latest offering in the City Lights Pocket Poets Series.
Lawrence Ferlinghetti discovered her
last year at the Winter Poetry Olympics in Calgary.
Word is she's been "working it" like mad,
winning over hardnosed, left-wing crowds
with her L.A. hipster, spoken word routine.

The reading's yet to begin: people are mingling
on the sidewalk, smoking, talking each
other up, faces gray in the shadowy
concrete dusk. Dennis introduces me
to a handsome, dark-haired man (I don't catch
his name), who I assume is with La Loca,
as he's standing close to her. "Great," I think,
"not only has she got a book from City Lights,
she's got a gorgeous boyfriend, too."

The audience files in. Dennis & Eileen
& I take seats in the first row, me between them.
When the handsome man I met outside
introduces the readers, I realize I was mistaken:
Oh, he's the curator of this series. But probably straight.
La Loca ("the crazy one") struts to the microphone
like a disaffected adolescent (she's thirty-nine):
skin pale, hair a bleached blonde

New Wave mess, black hiphuggers & boots.
She has an annoying Valley Girl affect.

Dennis, I can tell, is unimpressed:
he sits stiffly in his metal chair.
Eileen huffs & puffs throughout the reading,
miffed that the Pocket Poets Series,
which started with such luminaires
as Ginsberg & O'Hara, should end up publishing
this poseur, who came out of nowhere, & not herself.
I agree: La Loca is terrible. Sophomoric & high-
    pitched,
she's rambling on about some boy named Todd.
But having gotten sober in New Age L.A., I believe
(or am trying to, anyway) that good
can come from more than one source.

The next day, Dennis calls. It
turns out the handsome man (Ira) is
his publicist at Grove Press. Yes,
he also directs the literature program at
The Kitchen. No, he isn't straight.
"He thinks you're cute." "Really? I think
he's cute, too." Dennis audibly rolls his eyes;
all this cuteness appalls him. "I gave him
your phone number. Here's his."

Ira & I meet for dinner on a rainy, late September
weeknight. At a dark Mexican restaurant on Ninth
    Street.
"You can't get good Mexican food in this city,"
I say. "It's the thing I miss most about L.A."
He's ten years younger than I am, but seems
ten years older—a seasoned native New Yorker.
"A Jew from the Bronx" is how he refers to himself.

Both of us are relieved that the other smokes.
We agree to get together again,
after my Saturday morning meeting.
(I'm dissatisfied with New York A.A.
In L.A., everyone talks about God & working
the steps. Here they just complain
about their careers.) He's waiting for me
in the sunlight, on the southeast corner
of Tompkins Square Park, wearing a blue leather
jacket. He looks like a movie star: a younger
& shorter Richard Gere. But it's the blue
leather jacket that wins me. (I later
learn he borrowed it from one of his sisters.)

> Every month since
> we started dating,
> I've written a love
> poem for Ira. There
> are five so far. I
> show one to my
> poetry workshop
> at Brooklyn College.
> An airhead (who's
> gay, mind you) says
> it reads like a gay
> poem written for a
> straight audience.
> I am so ready for
> grad school to end.
>
> Ira unexpectedly
> comes by at lunch-
> time with a white
> Dean & DeLuca
> shopping bag: goat

cheese buttons (I
like the ones with
herbs better than
the ones with black
pepper), gourmet
crackers, a green bot-
tle of San Pellegrino,
a small container
of pasta salad. For
dessert: colorfully
iced flower-shaped
sugar cookies. We
picnic on the perma-
nently open futon,
make out for a bit.
I have a stack of stu-
dent papers to grade.
(I'm teaching a com-
position class.) He
has to get back to
his office to placate
an entitled author
on a reading tour.

Four a.m.: rowdy
partyers pour out
of The World across
the street, shouting
& breaking glass.
I wake & stumble to
the bathroom, half
remembering a bad
dream. Relentlessly,
the music in the next
apartment beats on

the wall behind Anne
Sexton. Unable to
fall asleep again, I
switch on the halo-
gen reading lamp
Ira bought me for
our six-month an-
niversary & write
a slender Schuyler-
esque poem about
"the noise surround-
ing me": the rowdy
partyers & the re-
lentless music & the
half-remembered
bad dream of my
own drinking. I
call it "The World."

Eileen encourages
me to memorize a
poem for my up-
coming reading at
A Different Light.
I am in awe of her
gutsy performance
style, so commit to
trying it. Readings
have always ter-
rified me; maybe
this might dispel my
stage fright. Since
it's the most recent,
I pick "The World."
Eileen listens to me

practice, gives me
tips, but on the night
of the reading I'm
a wreck. Afraid
I'll feel naked with-
out a script in my
hand. Afraid I'll
freeze if I make eye
contact with the
audience. Which
I watch trickle into
the small bookstore.
Raymond brings
Wieners; they sit
in the front row.
I'm excited, for all
my nervousness,
that the tatty, bril-
liantly mad John
Wieners will hear
me read. As I rise
to do so, he takes out
a crumpled pack of
Kents. Raymond
whispers that smok-
ing isn't allowed.
My spirit sinks as
Wieners gets up &
walks out. While I
recite "The World,"
I can see him stand-
ing outside the store:
ravaged face tilted
upward in profile &
cigarette pressed to

his lips, like a queen
of the silver screen.

I visit Kathe Burkhart in her studio in Brooklyn
(near the Williamsburg Bridge). We met when
we both lived in Los Angeles; I like
her work & her Morticia Addams look:
long, black, parted-down-the-middle hair,
black lipstick, all-black leather attire.
Under the table (i.e., at a cheaper
price than the gallery that represents her),
she sells me two of her pieces:
a black, glossily lacquered plaque
with a bustling New York street scene
& the white, handwritten caption
Someday I'll Live and Make Art Here
(which I must have as a good luck charm)
& a large painting from her *Liz Taylor Series*:
a primitive rendering of the actress
traced onto the canvas from a projected still
from *The Comedians* (a bomb with Richard Burton)
then painted in: her blouse turquoise, her eyes violet,
her bubble cut black, the revolver
she's aiming at someone off-canvas silver
(a tiny eight ball in its barrel; at first I missed it).
The title of the work stenciled above & below her
in lime green letters, on a brownish-red background:
What Comes Around Goes Around.
I feel this painting, with Liz on the verge
& its inverted proverb, will watch over me
in the years to come.

I boast that I am using my student loans to buy art
& take taxis, & in a sense it's true.
Less & less able to tolerate "the noise surrounding me,"

I'm spending more nights at Ira's apartment
in the East Seventies. He's given me my own key—
on a Tiffany key ring. In the morning
after he's left for work, I smoke, drink tea, grade papers
& listen, repeatedly, to his 10,000 Maniacs cassette.
I can't get enough of Natalie Merchant's plaintive
        voice & lyrics
& am especially fond of "Hey Jack Kerouac,"
the song Allen dislikes, perhaps because it
alludes to his sexuality. "I'm not a gay poet,"
he has told me. "I'm a political poet."

If I have an early class in Brooklyn, I don't
stay over; it's less of a trek from my place.
I leave Ira's around midnight & hail a cab downtown.
(Still self-conscious, I raise my arm tentatively,
consider it a near-miracle when a taxi actually stops.)
These are my most tranquil moments:
asking the driver if he minds if I smoke (they never do),
rolling the window down a crack,
flipping open the little metal ashtray
embedded in the armrest of the door,
lighting a cigarette with my red Bic,
relaxing into the first drag. "A quiet smoke in
a taxi is my idea of bliss," says Jimmy
in "A Few Days." Now I understand why.
There's nothing like it: speeding down
Second Avenue late at night, hardly any traffic,
hitting—if the driver times it just right—
only the green & yellow lights
all the way from the Upper East Side
to Alphabet City.

People here take me
seriously when I say
I'm a poet. They
don't crack jokes
like they do in L.A.

That alone makes
me think I might stay.

Commonplace

                    Each
has his "fiery particle"
to fan into flame for his own
sake.
            —James Schuyler

*

for that is life, to blaze with color

                —Alice Notley

*

one should go on till one's
hue is
unmistakeable

            —A.R. Ammons

*

"Not quite like anybody else."

                —James Schuyler

*

I am alone. As always. As all men.
With a magnificent obsession.

—John Wieners

*

one day
it is simply seen as a privilege,
to be one for long and so specifically
—how scary how exciting
a privilege—to expand to the fullness of the specific
one

—Alice Notley

*

to possess a bliss peculiar to each ones individual
existence

—John Keats

*

the color
about as great as color ever gets

—James Schuyler

*

Such a pink sky.

—Joe Brainard

*

after I have been
myself enough I will
die and go
on being universe

—A.R. Ammons

Elaine

for our birthdays

Was it mere coincidence
that we moved to New York
at the same time—you and Jerome
from Chicago, me from Los Angeles—
or was it predetermined, in our charts?
Born just four days apart
on either side of the cusp
between Cancer and Leo
(I'm the retiring crab, you
the self-possessed lion),
I've always pictured us waiting
in line, as for a roller coaster,
for our current incarnations to begin.
I board first: "See you in twenty-seven
Earth years in Venice, California, U.S.A."
And so it came to be that in 1980
we met in human form when Dennis
brought you and Jerome to read
at Beyond Baroque. His Little Caesar anthology
*Coming Attractions: American Poets
in Their Twenties* had finally come out.
I'd waited half an Earth year for that
book to appear. Quite
excruciating. I thought it
would change my life
dramatically. It didn't.
But some important relationships
came from it: Dennis, Tim, Eileen, you.
I recognized you immediately:
short auburn hair and elfin face (made up
with thick mascara and plum lipstick). Stylishly

gaunt, androgynous, you wore a long-sleeved
black-and-white-striped Breton tee—
like Andy and Edie, like Debbie Harry, like James
    Dean.
Hip, but not at all pretentious—
a theatrical cross between beatnik and punk.
In Chicago, at the Museum of Contemporary Art,
you and Jerome had disrupted
a Creeley reading by raunchily
carrying on in the audience—
as if, one witness complained in print,
you were in a motel room.
Your unrepentant reply: "Since we fucked
in the john so many times in the past
and found the stalls very accommodating,
we'd thought we'd give the main floor a try."

That night at Beyond Baroque,
Jerome was so drunk he could
barely stand. I'd never seen anyone
that wasted perform in public.
You followed: smart, angular, mischievous, witty.
Your poems full of Barbie dolls, cosmetics, Big Macs.
I beamed through your entire reading.
Afterwards, you told me my smile
anchored you. A year or two
later, when Dennis published
Shrewcrazy, you came back.
Jerome was newly sober;
I can still see him sitting,
shell-shocked, on the small blue sofa
in my cave-like studio apartment in Hollywood.
During a party at Jack Skelley's,
you and I snuck off, locked
the bathroom door, snorted coke.

A couple of years after that,
when *I* was newly sober, you
set up a reading for me at Links Hall
in Chicago. As I read
my TV haiku, someone said
to you: "I can see why you like
his poems so much." I wrote
a new one that trip, for you,
about being in your home:
drinking Constant Comment
with milk and honey, smoking
cigarettes, listening to the soundtrack
to *Vertigo*, looking at your books
and art and the sunlight
coming through your red mini-blinds
in stripes on the hardwood floor.

More time passed on the material plane.
Then, in the year 1988, as ordained
by the stars, we both, unbeknownst
to each other, made plans
to move to New York in July.
One of the first things I did after I arrived
was make a beeline for your building
on Mulberry Street. I couldn't breathe
I was so excited, waiting for the doorman
to announce me, couldn't believe we were together—
I *knew* our friendship would flourish—
in this hot, dirty, fast-paced place
where I hoped to broaden my experiences and my art.
You gave me, as a welcome gift,
your copy of *The Crystal Lithium*,
the only Schuyler volume I didn't own.
Such a generous gesture—
the book was long out of print

and impossible, pre-Internet, to find—
I've never forgotten it.
I asked Jimmy to sign it the next time
I visited him at the Chelsea.
"Love in New York," he inscribed.
(There would be love for me in New York,
as well as deep disappointment and grief,
which you would witness
and help guide me through.)
I see us huddled together,
the "new kids" in town,
at crowded parties, at poetry readings
at St. Mark's, and under my
first three-dollar New York umbrella
outside the Ear Inn. Jerome
can't quite fit: his first black
New York turtleneck glistens
with drops of rain. Beneath
the green awning, Eileen
and Barbara chat with a woman
in a tan hat. When they're finished,
we all five pile into a
cab. Cramped between Jerome
and the door, I have trouble
getting my umbrella to snap shut.

The above scene is lifted from
a bad poem I wrote that September.
I diligently chronicle every detail—
except who we'd just heard read
and which restaurant the cab was taking us to.
How smitten I was (and still am) with
the mundaneness of the moment. So New York
    School.

I see you and me meeting
in the East Village, at Veselka.
The first of innumerable times.
Nestled at a table against
the wall, we order vegetable soup
and challah bread, cheese and potato pierogies.
A blueberry muffin, always, to go.
(David Shapiro once joined us there and
held us hostage while he talked nonstop.)
And eating, often, at 2nd Ave Deli:
matzah ball soup and pastrami (lean) on rye
with French fries and a Dr. Brown's cream soda.
If lucky, we were seated in the Molly Picon room.
I see us sitting on a bench
in an open courtyard on 63rd Street
savoring lemon cake and sipping
Earl Grey tea and smoking lots
of cigarettes before teaching
our workshops at the West Side Y.
I see you sitting and smoking with Joe Brainard
at a dinner party at Ira's and my loft.
I remember this, I suppose, because
I wanted to sit and smoke with the two of you,
but had to play "hostess."

Out of the blue I recall that
you once found a wad of cash—
hundreds of dollars—
in the back seat of a cab.
And that you thought the lucky pennies
in New York were too dirty to pick up.

There's a picture of us online
taken by John Tranter in 1992.
You had a breakfast date with him and his wife

Lyn, and invited me along.
It captures us after our meal,
outside Spring Street Natural.
Frigid morning: Lafayette Street
a blur of mauve, green, and gray.
Lyn is pulling a black glove
onto her right hand. You and I
stand apart. Open
to the camera, you look as if you're
stepping toward it. A fish brooch
("made from a tiny freeze-dried shad
in transparent plastic," Tranter explains
on his website) leaps upward
on your black coat. You hold
a black Ferragamo purse. I suppress
a smile as I squint, puffy-eyed, and take
a drag on my ever-present cigarette.
The three buttons on my green tweed coat,
like your brooch, catch the winter light.
Black scarf wrapped around my neck.
Gray beginning to show in my hair.

I see (thanks to one of your poems)
us standing, several years later,
in the little alley behind
the Puck Building (across
from the Pop Shop), staring up
at a sudden fluttering of pink shutters—
the whole side of the building alive
with them—our spirits rising
to the sunlit pink wing-tips at the top.
I still haven't come down from that flight!
When I told you I preferred
to read your books on airplanes,
you signed your next one

"more 'in-flight' reading."
I saved it for my next trip.

So many rides! Planes
with your poems tucked
in the seat pocket till
after takeoff, cabs
with gratuitous wads of cash
in the back seat.

And before we knew it, fourteen years—
two full life cycles—had passed.
I'd met Ira, lived with him
for ten years, then spent two
climbing the pale green walls of my SoHo loft
trying to figure out what to do
next. I desperately wanted
out of New York. But where to go?
Los Angeles was no longer home:
that door had shut years before.
Blessedly a new one finally opened
and I moved to Chicago—
your former home—to teach
at Columbia College—your alma mater.
We marveled at this unforeseen
twist of events (divinely designed,
no doubt). The distance
only deepened our friendship.
Long, intimate telephone calls.
Postcards with your good wishes
neatly printed in green ink.
Intense visits (as when we first
knew one another) when poetry brings me
to your city, or you to mine. *So many rides!*

And now we are about to turn sixty!
How can this be? "I think it calls for a purse,"
you said when we pondered it.
Dear Elaine, that we've been friends
for more than half our lives
pleases me no end.
May we continue to dedicate poems
to each other, continue to counsel
one another and confide in each other,
continue to share our good days and our bad days
for the rest of this incarnation—
and beyond. You recently remarked
that you want to be a businessman
in your next life. I don't
know if that would suit me.
Would you consider toymaker?
tightrope walker? game show panelist?
I trust we'll have plenty of time to decide
as we wait in line for the next ride.

Joe

When you came to a dinner party at
Ira's and my loft, you brought
a lemon tart. Elaine remembers
this, I don't. You once said
"You can't beat meat, potatoes
and a green vegetable"
but not to me: Jimmy quotes
you in one of his uncollected poems,
"Within the Dome." And calls you
"the great Joe Brainard"
(which indeed you were). I was
well aware of that as I sat
across from you in a dim restaurant
in Tribeca—the first time, though
I'd met you six years earlier, that we
actually had a meal together.
It was such an honor to know you,
Joe, you'd think I'd remember
more about you than I do.
Friendly face. Swept-back, silvering
hair. Gold glints (lit match to
cigarette) in your round glasses.
Expensive white dress shirt
unbuttoned halfway down your
tanned (and hairy) chest. Shy
but in command, you reached for
the check. My best memories
have already gone into another poem.
How at a crowded party on
Washington Mews, during a
snowstorm, you towered over me

(I was sitting on the staircase, smoking)
and told me how attractive I looked
in my black sweater. How we
once almost had sex. "Can I
take you to dinner?" you wrote.
"And why don't you bring a
toothbrush with you and plan
on spending the night." I did
plan on it, but you caught a cold,
couldn't keep our date. And
never dropped the hint again.
How when Eileen was directing
the Poetry Project, she paired me
with Lyn Hejinian (something
perverse there). That was a tough
reading. When Alice, whom I
revered, walked in, I exclaimed,
"I'm so glad you came!" Startled,
she said, "I came to hear Lyn."
As did the majority of the audience.
My usually crowd-pleasing Supremes
poem was met with stony indifference.
Yet when I was able to look up
from my book (and that took
courage, believe me), I saw you
sitting in the middle of the room,
a broad smile across your face.
Everyone always speculated, Joe,
as to why you stopped making art—
the thought of *not* producing
inconceivable to the ambitious
throng of New York School wannabes.
Had you burnt out on speed
in the seventies? Been turned off

by the rise of commercialism in
the eighties? Or did you simply
feel (again inconceivable) that
you'd accomplished enough?
After you died, it became apparent
that this was, in fact, the case:
you left behind not one, but two
substantial bodies of work—
visual art *and* writing. And
produced classics in both genres—
with hardly anybody noticing.
They think only of themselves
and brag about what they do.
Your *Collected Writings*, its
powder blue dust jacket dotted
with your childlike gold stars,
is, almost twenty years after
your death, a joy to hold. Was
it a dream? Were we really friends?
I only visited you once, that I
can remember, in your loft on
Greene Street. Toward the end.
Not one bit of art on the white
walls, and next to no furniture—
had you always lived so sparely?
Nowhere to sit, let alone linger.
You weren't doing much, you said,
except reading (the novels you'd
recently devoured were stacked
near the door; I brought you
some that Ira had published),
smoking your eight (or was it
nine?) requisite cigarettes per day,
and occasionally dressing up

for dinners (which you, I'm sure,
paid for) with devoted friends.
Can one have too many of those?
You seemed to, and so, as you
weakened, dressed up even less.

Acker is back in New York

after living in London
for most of the eighties,
where her post-punk rewrites
of classics like *Great Expectations*
and *Don Quixote* earned her
the title of "literary terrorist"
and *Blood and Guts in High School*
put her on the map in a big way,
and everyone is complaining
about her: *She's changed. She's
too much of a narcissist. She wasn't
this bad when she lived in New York.
Success has gone to her head.*
I have nothing invested in this
debate, have never met or read
Acker, so I find it interesting
that they're in such a tizzy.
"It's all about *her*," whines Gary
with a listless, effeminate hand-wave,
letting his cigarette ash drop
on our new carpet. He's one
mean, bitter little queen. As
much as I like his work, I can't,
now that I know him, read him
anymore. "This just isn't *her*,"
opines Lynne, fingering her pointy
chin, then shaking, to convey
incredulousness, her clown-like
frizz of dyed-black hair. Lynne's
habit of whipping the cover
of her latest book out of her purse
every time you bump into her

has made her the butt of an
oft-told joke. I promise myself
that if I ever have as many books
as she does, I'll be grateful and
not harp about other writers.
Fame, fame, fatal fame. It's what
everyone wants. But God
help you if you become more
famous than your friends.

I finally meet Acker (no one
calls her Kathy) at a party
celebrating Ira's new literary
agency. She's every inch the
outlaw. Bleached-blonde hair
cut concentration-camp short.
Ears pierced many times over.
Tight black spaghetti-strap top
prominently displaying the birds,
flowers, and koi tattooed across
her arms and back. I'm more
impressed to meet Jenny Plath,
Sylvia's niece, who works in
publishing. And upset when
Ira's tall, good-looking intern
from Grove Press, in the middle of
making chitchat, looks down
at me and says, "I'm going
to take Ira away from you."
Ira's a little too flattered when
I tell him about it afterwards,
and not nearly reassuring enough,
which only irks me further.

Of course Ira, who's known
as a star-maker, has no problem
with Acker's notoriety. As her
publicist, he's traveled with
her on tour, thinks of her as
an older sister. I listen to
them talk shop. I'm the silent
"wife"—nascent, no threat.
I smoke and worry about my
next poem: *Where will it come
from?* Their talk, which I only
half hear, is all about her. Why
shouldn't it be. She's famous.

Acker doesn't stick around
New York for long. She sells
her loft on 12th Street and
hightails it to San Francisco.
Where else do the mavericks go?
When *High Risk* comes out,
Ira arranges for us to read
together at A Different Light
in the Castro. Acker pulls up
in front of the bookstore on her
motorcycle, sporting a black
leather jacket (with red rose
airbrushed on the back), some
sort of high-fashion white tutu
and tights, and combat boots
with silver-studded heels
and toes. Instead of our own
work, we read pieces by
contributors who have died
of AIDS. I read Cookie Mueller's
story about a "golden showers

guy, a man into water sports,
a pee hag"; Acker dramatically
delivers Manuel Ramos Otero's
"The Exemplary Life of the
Slave and the Master": "spit
in my face . . . put your whole
fist inside me . . . plunge your
pointed tongue into the abyss
that I am." On another trip,
when Ira and I pick her up
to take her to dinner, Acker's
listening to Patti Smith's *Horses*
as she dons her designer gear:
a black lambskin jacket with
shaggy pink fur on the collar
and cuffs. We step around
pages of the novel she's trying
to finish, *My Mother: Demonology*,
strewn all over the floor.

The last time I see her is in
New York. For Ira's birthday,
she takes us to see Edward
Albee's *Three Tall Women*. It
makes sense that she likes
Albee, another writer with
mother issues. People gawk
at her Hells Angels/prima
ballerina drag—how can they
not? She's remade herself
into a spectacle (the most
wounded among us do).

Acker's death, at fifty, hard
for Ira, simply makes me sad.
An insult, after all the AIDS
deaths, and Jimmy's, and Bob
Flanagan's, and my mother's,
from cancer, the previous year.
I spent time with Acker, but
never really got to know
her. At the first reading I
give after her death, I read
D.H. Lawrence's "The End,
the Beginning" in her honor:
"once dipped in dark oblivion
the soul has peace, inward
and lovely peace." The next
time I fly to Los Angeles, I
ask Helen, my psychic, about
Acker. Helen rubs her fingers
together, tunes into the other
world, and all but gasps: "Oh,
her transition was *magnificent*."
I make note of it, but don't
tell anyone when I get back to
New York, for fear her friends
might envy her even that.

Tim

When you came to a dinner party at
Ira's and my loft, you brought
a fruit tart. A glazed kaleidoscope
of peach, kiwi, and strawberry slices.
It was an auspicious occasion:
dinner with James Schuyler.
You'd always been a fan of his work.
Jimmy, on the other hand, had never
been impressed by yours. ("I do not share
your enthusiasm for Dlugos," he wrote
in a letter in 1985.) But he had
read and been wowed by "G-9,"
your long poem about having AIDS,
just out in *The Paris Review*,
and now wanted to meet you.
August 9, 1990. (I'm glad I saved
my datebooks.) Jimmy eventually
made it up two flights—quite a feat
considering his heft and bad leg.
Inside the loft, he almost slipped on
one of Ira's throw rugs. The rest
of the evening I worried that he might
fall and hurt himself. I sat with
you and Christopher (your last lover)
and Jimmy, smoking and listening
(small talk—nothing memorable),
a rather sullen host, while Ira
threw together a salad and his
specialty pasta dish in the kitchen.
Worried, too, about your gaunt
appearance, the little round Band-Aid
covering a KS lesion on your cheek.

Thinking back on it, I see how
deeply into myself I had retreated.
People were dying and no one seemed
to be talking about what mattered.
In less than four months, you would
be gone. Jimmy would join you
in the afterlife the following April.
Ever courteous, you sent a card
thanking us for "a lovely evening
of great food, conversation, and
friendship. It was wonderful to be
able to spend time with Jimmy
(is it okay to call him by his first name,
gulp?), who seemed very happy, too."
I'll trust, at this late date, that this
is true. I saved everything you ever
sent me, Tim, every letter, poem, post
and Christmas card, thank you note.
This one had gooseberries on it—
twelve of George Brookshaw's veined,
alien-looking green and red orbs—
rendered with impeccable detail.
All these years, I've held onto the copy
of *Tanaquil*—the novel by Donald
Windham—you gave me. When
you came across a stack of them
at the Strand, it pained you to see
your friend's book—you loved
both, your friend and his book—
on the remainder pile, so you bought
them all and presented them to friends.
I confess I still haven't read it.
Will I ever? The glue in the spine
is dried out. Two decades after
your death, when I was editing

your collected poems, I got in touch
with your brother John. A building
supervisor for the phone company
in Washington, D.C. Parents and only
sibling (you'd both been adopted)
long dead, single since his divorce
in the seventies. "I'm a nice guy,"
he admitted, "but I'm miserable."
He also admitted he was pissed off
when you got AIDS. (He was
with you on G-9 when you died.)
The implication: you should have
been more careful, restrained yourself.
He had all of your childhood ephemera:
photographs of you (a skinny
kid with glasses) and the family,
report cards (you were a straight-A
student), a program for a piano
recital (on June 14, 1962, you played
"The Parade of the Wooden Soldiers"),
two religious medals, your Roy Rogers
and Dale Evans lunchbox (with
"Francis Dlugos" written in pencil
and "Remember: thou shalt not steal")
filled with commemorative stamps
and political buttons: Nixon, Goldwater,
LBJ, JFK. If I came to visit him,
John told me, he would let me take
whatever I wanted. I intended to,
but waited too long. The next time
I tried to contact him, his number had
been disconnected. After some
detective work, I discovered that
John A. Dlugos (nicknamed "Doogee")
had died unexpectedly in his sleep.

"He was preceded in death by
his parents and brother Timothy,
a published poet." Survived by
"adoring friends too numerous to
count." I'll trust that this is true.
No will. A cousin was contacted by
the attorney, but wanted nothing.
All of the possessions—including
your mother's cedar chest and a quilt
she made, which John had retrieved
from your apartment in New Haven
upon your death—disposed of,
given away. Tim, I mourned your
lost memorabilia. Kicked myself
for not jumping on John's offer.
But where else can what's been lost
live, save in the poem. Nine
months before you were lifted into
the afterlife, you organized a reading
for us at Yale Divinity School. On
the flyer, next to "New York poets!"
and our names, you put a picture
of the Everly Brothers in a somewhat
fey (how appropriate) pose, singing
their hearts out. Only three people
showed up. But we sang our
hearts out anyway. We had agreed
to introduce each other. I wasn't
happy with what I wrote—dashed
off on your electric typewriter shortly
before. In the Institute of Sacred
Music's nearly empty Great Hall, you
praised my work for "its unflinching
willingness to share disquieting
emotions like shame and regret,

as well as the real-life situations
that provoked them." And: "David's
poetry pays careful attention to
the *things* of ordinary life—the concrete
details which might be overlooked
by poets who foreground their
strong feelings at the expense of
the evanescent or ephemeral."
And: "I admire his work more
than he knows." Moved, I asked
you, afterwards, for a copy. You
handed me the one you'd read.
Which I asked you to autograph.
Almost posthumous, you wrote:
"This proves I really *did* write
the foregoing!" I, heartsick to be
losing you, needed proof. I would
have been too desolate without it.

From a Notebook

First she referred to my lover as your little bastard boyfriend and I said I think that's a hostile thing to say and she said I knew by your silence that you disapproved but it's just the way I talk I meant it affectionately to which I responded I can't believe there isn't any hostility behind a statement like that to which she responded you know there's really a class difference here and I said what and she said it's an east coast/west coast thing and I said east coast/west coast it's inappropriate and then she said something about male bonding vs. female bonding and how she was finally giving herself permission to have fights and I tried to point out how her competitiveness was interfering with our relationship and somewhere in there she said you don't have anything I want and I said at this point in my life I need friends around me who are capable of mutual respect and support and to be honest I just don't trust you right now and then there was a long pause and then she said that really hurt.

1/18/91

I called Eileen

to tell her Tim had died.
We'd both visited him on G-9
in the weeks previous,
part of the sad procession
of friends and family who came
to sit vigil and say (without saying
it) goodbye. One of the last
things he said to me was
"Will you look after my work?"
"Yes, of course," I replied. "You
don't even have to ask." Jane,
who was with him when he passed,
said at one point Tim said to her,
"Can you please remove this torpor?"
meaning the numbness of the drugs—
he wanted to be conscious
of what he was experiencing.
Jane had been there when he learned
he was dying. "Oh, so my lifespan
is weeks instead of months?"
His female doctor had cried.
I couldn't, three days after he died,
sitting next to Ira in the second-to-last pew
in the Church of St. Mary the Virgin
on 46th Street, as a multitude
of gay men filed in. One queen
feigned shock at seeing all his
tricks in the daylight. I refused to
laugh, though there was truth
in it: a palpable sense that most of
the mourners had spent time with
each other in dark, clandestine places.

The service I endured by staring
at the back of the head directly in
front of me. For months I was numb.
Sat, late at night, sifting through
Tim's papers. (Christopher had
promptly delivered them to me.) It
seemed so little—his whole life
reduced to four or five cardboard
boxes. And yet those boxes contained
hundreds of poems, largely unpublished,
and his whole life lay hidden in them.
Poems painful to read, to handle,
spread out across the floor then put
in order by year. Some—the ones
he wrote at the end, his death sentence
imbued with such hopefulness—
I retyped and submitted to magazines.
In the midst of this process, Eileen
published an account, in her column
in *Paper*, of her last visit with Tim.
She'd complained to him, once again,
about not being in *High Risk*, the anthology
that all but ruined our friendship.
(She turned on me when Ira, whom
I was dating, flatly refused to include her.)
"Oh Eileen," said Tim, "let it go."
Infuriated, I dashed off a note
telling her how disappointing it was
to hear that she had troubled our
dear friend on his deathbed with
her petty resentment. She sent my
note back. On it, she'd scrawled
a message, something to the effect
that I wasn't very intelligent. I
tore it to bits and returned it to her—

an envelope of furious confetti.
Our quarrel made it into a poem
of Tom's, "Collateral Damage":
"Eileen and David are still fighting."
Four and a half months later, we'd
patched things up enough that

Eileen called me to tell me
Jimmy had died. She sounded
almost gleeful. "Well, I have
more people to call. Bye!"
We'd both visited him at St. Vincent's
the week after his stroke,
part of the procession of poets
who came to pay him homage.
I ran into Douglas Crase
in the lobby: he was leaving
as I was coming in. He made light
of our meeting like this, perhaps
because I looked so frightened.
At the desk they handed me a visitor's pass
and directed me to intensive care.
A shock to see Jimmy: rotund
in his hospital gown, unable to talk,
eyes searching mine—for what?
No hiding the distress in my face.
I didn't know what to say—no different
from the hours I'd spent with him
in his room at the Chelsea Hotel
(to which he would never return).
My eyes kept gravitating toward
his bare feet, his several missing toes.
Darragh leaned against the wall
the whole time, arms sternly crossed.
Why didn't he leave us alone? I

might have felt more comfortable
without his watchful presence, been able
to speak freely to Jimmy. As I was
leaving, Anne Porter, her white hair
pulled back into a grandmotherly bun,
came in. She was, in fact, Jimmy's
last visitor. Darragh sprang to life:
"Oh, Anne . . ." Fairfield's widow—
how perfect. As if he were a director
and this the unexpected scene he needed
to finish his film. He ushered her
to the side of Jimmy's bed. Cut to
the exterior of the Church of the
Incarnation on Madison Avenue,
after Jimmy's funeral. I tried to hug
Darragh, but his stiffness rebuked me.
(Later I learned Ann Lauterbach
had the same experience I did. In
the wake of Jimmy's death, Darragh
locked himself in Jimmy's room
at the Chelsea and drew everything
in it, even its absent tenant. This
led Doug to dub him "the widow
Park." Darragh's own death awaited
him eighteen years in the future:
blind and starting to lose his mind,
he, as Tom described it, "blew his
brains out." It made me sad, though
not for the reason one might expect;
I never understood why he took a dislike
to me. How many, when my day
comes, will have such mixed feelings?)
Eileen and I, face to face, in front
of the church. Did either of us
attempt a hug? "I can't believe

Jimmy's gone," I said. "Yeah,"
she responded, "it's our turn now."
I knew in that instant that we
would never again be friends.
Suddenly we were alone—where
did everyone vanish to? But
it had always felt like that when
I was with her, that feeling
reserved for lovers: like we were
the only two people in the world.
We required separate cabs. She was off
to a post-service supper (invitation
only) hosted by Darragh. Who
else had been invited? Raymond?
Tom? It didn't matter, not really.
I was going to have to learn
to be alone with my grief.
She took the first taxi; I watched
it drive up Madison and make
a right on 36th Street. Then turned
around and, to flag the second one,
numbly held out my hand.

III

Three Tall Women

Anaïs

is writing in her diary on the train
that takes her to and from Paris, the shaky
little antiquated train that always makes
her think of Proust. It shakes words, phrases,
insights from her teeming mind
into her constantly moving pen
as the glow of the city recedes
in the fogged-up window. She is feverish
with excitement, returning from another adventure
with Henry and June. She must get it all down
lest it be lost, swallowed by the black
vacuum of passing time. Both of them
obsess her. Henry, genius of the lower depths,
who is writing a book, *Tropic of Cancer*,
that will shock the world with its
brutality and raw sexuality, a book
full of everything other novels leave out—
the pain and mystery of real experience.
He had no typewriter, so she gave him hers.
Now she reads the pages as he unwinds them,
swooning at the power of his vital, violent words.
June, his second wife, who has arrived
from New York, only to beguile both Henry
and Anaïs. To love June is to enter a labyrinth
of contradictions and lies. Yet she is
the most beautiful woman Anaïs
has ever seen. Startlingly white face
and burning eyes. Blonde hair piled high,
carelessly, about to topple. Endlessly
fidgeting, lighting cigarettes, creating
a smoke screen of self-dramatizing tales.
Anaïs relishes the hole in her black stockings,

her red velvet dress. She feels drawn to her
as towards death. Tonight, she offered up
her cape, wrapped it around June's incandescent
skin. In return, June gave Anaïs her silver bracelet—
a precious gift. It clutches her wrist
now, like June's very fingers, as she writes
in her diary. The shaky little Proustian
train lets out a whistle and comes to a stop.
Her footsteps echo through the cobblestone
streets of Louveciennes. Dogs bark.
The green gate creaks, the gravel driveway
crunches under her feet. She throws open
her bedroom window and breathes
the smell of wet leaves. Each room
of her house is painted a different color,
as if there were one room for every separate mood:
red for passion, peach for gentleness, green for repose.
This one is pale turquoise—for reveries.

At nineteen, I read all of Nin's diaries,
volume one through four (as many as were
published at that point), one after the other—
the quintessential Anaïs addict. Each volume
bore the same dreamy headshot of her
on the cover, tinted a different color, like the rooms
of her home in Louveciennes, like flavors
of candy. Volume one (pink) was Henry and June
in Paris in the early thirties, psychoanalysis
with Allendy and Rank, the madness
of Artaud. Volume two (blue) was Gonzalo
and his neurotic wife Helba; *La Belle Aurore*,
the houseboat in which Nin lived on the Seine;
young Lawrence Durrell. Volumes three
and four (amber and green) were her years
in New York during the war: setting up

a printing press (after constant rejection) to
publish her fiction, writing erotica for one dollar
per page, recording the secrets of her famous friends:
poet Robert Duncan, actress Luise Rainer,
critic Edmund Wilson, novelist Gore Vidal.
Through it all she sacrificed, suffered
lack of attention, but ultimately triumphed
in the mid-sixties, when her diaries were published
to great acclaim. Anaïs became my muse,
my spiritual mother (she had the same sign
as my mother: Pisces), my first literary idol.
How else could I, a baby boomer in the suburbs
of Los Angeles, have learned what it means
to be an artist. Her diaries taught me
how I wanted to lead my life: cultivating
stimulating relationships with other writers,
ever evolving and maintaining my integrity
as a human being, valuing my own experiences
as the stuff of art. *The personal life deeply lived
always expands into truths beyond itself.* That was
practically all I needed to know, the motto
with which I would venture forth.

In the fall of 1973 (I was now twenty),
I went with my friend Jenny (an artist
who'd turned me onto the diaries; she later
became a well-known punk rock photographer)
to see two Bergman films at an art house
on Wilshire Boulevard. Anaïs was exiting
the lobby as we arrived. She wore
her signature black cape and a pendant
of a fiery gold sun, her long auburn hair
in a bohemian bun, and was escorted by
handsome Rupert Pole. Jenny screamed
and ran up to them. I stood back, in stunned

awe. She told Jenny she'd just reseen
Persona for an upcoming lecture on Bergman
at UCLA. Impossible to concentrate
on the movies (Bergman was difficult enough
under normal circumstances) with the image
of Anaïs in my mind: poised and gracious
and larger than life. Late that night,
I wrote a fan letter and sent it (Jenny
had her address, a P.O. box in Los Angeles)
with one of my recent poems. I identified
myself as the young man in front of the theater
and admitted I'd been too shy to approach her.
I felt certain she would write to me: she claimed,
in interviews, that she answered all her
fan mail because she'd been hurt, when young,
that her first fan letter, to *Nightwood* author
Djuna Barnes, went without a response.
I waited expectantly—weeks and weeks.
Finally, a purple postcard fell through
the mail slot in my parents' front door.
She'd answered! A sweet, encouraging
handwritten message. (I stared at my
name in her delicate, slanted hand.) She
thanked me for my letter and commented on
my poem. I'd captured, in so few words,
she said, the theme of her entire diary—
the lack of a father's love. Extremely generous
of her, considering it was the effort of a beginner.
Her reply meant the world to me. She'd
given me her blessing. I could, would be a writer.
"Let me know, later, how it goes," she wrote.
Sadly, I wasn't able to: she died six months
before I published my first poem.

I kept up with the diaries as they appeared:
volume five (copper) in 1974, volume six (red)
in 1976. I missed volume seven (silver) completely.
By that time (1980), I'd "outgrown" Anaïs,
which is to say I'd moved on to other influences:
Ann Stanford and May Swenson; Sexton,
Plath and Hughes; the Ginsberg of "Kaddish";
the Elizabeth Bishop of *Geography III*. And soon
the more intimate poets of the New York School:
O'Hara, Schuyler, Brainard, Berrigan, the Notley
of *Waltzing Matilda* and *How Spring Comes*. But my
love of autobiography can be traced, fondly,
to Anaïs. I did read *Henry and June* in
1988, on the verge of moving to New York.
It came as a surprise to me that she and Henry
were lovers; I was a naive nineteen. A good thing,
probably. If I had read the unexpurgated diary
then, it might have inspired me to be more
adventurous, sexually, and I would be dead
of AIDS. *I want more than ever to fuck and to be fucked* . . .
I might have adopted that as my motto.
Where will Anaïs hide her diary tonight?
In a hole in the mattress? In the stove with the ashes?
It would hurt Hugo, her loyal husband, if he
were to read of her exploits. And sadden him,
surely, to learn that his wife prefers
Henry's penis to his own: *Hugo is sexually*
too large for me . . . always somewhat painful.
Whereas Henry's medium-sized cock
brought her to 1001 climaxes. Anaïs
went so far as to fill her diary with lies
to cover her infidelity. *To love her was*
to enter a labyrinth of . . . The biggest
one I ever saw (and touched) was in the labyrinth
of the Club Baths in San Francisco in 1976.

A short Hispanic (in those days
I would have said "Mexican") man
cornered me in the orgy room, wanted me
to come with him to his private cubicle.
I wanted romance more than raw sex—
absurd to expect that at the bars or baths
or in the parks, though I found it exciting to wander
after midnight among mist-shrouded trees
and get a blowjob in the bushes.
The men in relationships were all cheating
on each other, anyway. And I was guarded.
(I had, after all, been raped.) That little horse-hung
guy tried his best to convince me. But there
was no way I was going to let him get me alone.

Ann Stanford stood at the blackboard

in a classroom flooded with California sunlight,
spring 1972, reciting a poem by E.A. Robinson:
"And Richard Cory, one calm summer night,
Went home and put a bullet through his head."

I sat in the aisle closest to the open windows
smoking a Marlboro 100. (You could smoke
anywhere in those days.) What would I have
been wearing? Brown corduroy jeans. Brown

and pink baseball T-shirt (with three-quarter
sleeves)—a statement on color, not the sport.
Two-tone (caramel and brown) tennis shoes.
My hair—black, shoulder-length—was cut in

a shag like Jane Fonda, my anti-establishment
idol, in *Klute*, which I'd seen innumerable times.
I'd lost weight since high school (the stress of
entering college—San Fernando Valley State,

soon renamed Cal State Northridge), smoked
more now that I didn't have to hide it. Eighteen,
and no clue what I would do with my life. No
idea I would spend it writing poems, like my

Introduction to Literature teacher. I didn't in
fact know that she was a famous poet. I only
knew something nebulous inside me had to
find artistic expression. Outside: birdsong,

the orange-popsicle beaks of birds-of-paradise
in the campus planters. I understood the theme
of "Richard Cory": that what we're conditioned
to want—property, money, prestige—doesn't

necessarily make us happy, that even the most
privileged among us can quietly suffer, take
their own lives. But was too shy to raise my
hand. What did she see in me that I couldn't

see in myself? Intelligence? Determination?
A spark of talent? She praised my writing
(though chided me for my poor spelling). It
took so little: her minimal, penciled comments

(*I like this!*) were enough to make me believe I
might really be able to write. She seemed wise
and kind, and was tolerant, but only to a point:
"You mean poetry doesn't pay?" some jock

balked in workshop. "What good is it, then?"
"If you want to make money," she shot back,
pointing at the door, "go do something else.
You won't get rich writing poems." That was

all right with me—I'd read "Richard Cory."
An unworldly profession wouldn't please my
parents (no health benefits). What else could I
do but sit in the stacks at the school library and

pore over her poems. "The Sleeping Princess"
shocked me. It said I would wake up one day
and be old. Unthinkable, yet it had to be true.
(I am older now, writing this, than she was

when I first met her.) Every week, she sat with
us in the workshop circle, her full head of hair
silver in the incessant suburban light. A hint of
Asia in her face, around the eyes. She always

wore muted earth tones (it was the seventies):
beige blouse, green and brown plaid pants.
And preppy blazer when she gave readings—
poets should look their best at the podium.

When her poems appeared in *The New Yorker*
(which they did regularly), students buzzed.
I tore them out and hole-punched them into
my black three-ring binder of "special poems,"

reread them till I knew them by heart. (I can
still quote them to this day.) I often visited
during her office hours (on the seventh floor
of monolithic Sierra Tower). Once, she was

eating lunch: sliced avocado (her family had
an orchard south of Los Angeles) on yellow
bread. (Why is this the detail I remember?)
One time I ran into her outside, stopped to

say hi. The woman standing with her made
a catty remark about demanding students.
 "Oh, David is a wonderful writer," Ann said.
Had anyone ever stood up for me like that?

On a balmy evening, fall 1977, I stood alone at
a reception for her new book, *In Mediterranean
Air*, at a store near school. After she read (in
her blazer), I feigned interest in the bestsellers,

waited until the crowd dispersed to have her
sign my copy. "For a fine poet & friend," she
wrote. Me, a fine poet! She'd confirmed it, in
blue ink (which matched, perfectly, the color

of the cover). And I was more than a student—
I was her friend. How could I, floating out of
the bookshop and across the parking lot, high
on her inscription and the free white wine, the

Southern California air indeed Mediterranean,
twilight a smoggy orange-gray parfait above
the drive-through Wells Fargo on the corner
of Nordhoff and Reseda, have foreseen Ann's

fate: a decade later she would die, at seventy,
of liver cancer. I called her sometime that last
year, not knowing she was ill, to ask if she'd
recommend me for a Guggenheim fellowship.

Yes, was her answer, though she stressed she
had never received one herself. (I didn't, in
the end, apply.) Poetry was not foremost on
her mind, she told me; in fact, whenever her

poems appeared in print, she simply tossed
the publications into a closet. Since retiring
from teaching, she'd spent much of her time
gardening and reading mysteries. I attended

her memorial service with Eloise Klein Healy,
in white July heat, five days after my birthday
(I'd turned thirty-four). Church of the Hills,
Forest Lawn. James Krusoe sat a few pews

in front of us. We asked him to move back.
Jim was cryptic: tall and slim; wiry, graying
hair and bushy eyebrows; a knowing sadness
engrained in his face. He wore his trademark

blue work shirt (and, out of respect, a tie and
tweed jacket). Something somberly classical—
Brahms?—was played. Then Rosanna, one of
Ann's three daughters, approached the pulpit

and spoke. She quoted a letter May Swenson,
Ann's longtime friend, had written when she
learned Ann was close to death. How could I,
numbly listening to the words (I wouldn't truly

feel grief until my mother died), have foreseen
that a decade later all of Ann's books would be
out of print; that to rectify this, I would team
up with Maxine Scates, who'd studied with

Ann before I did, and edit her selected poems.
Two true former students who met in person
for the first time at the Huntington Library in
San Marino, California (I flew to Los Angeles

from Manhattan, where I'd moved the year
after Ann died; Maxine drove down the coast
from Oregon), to sit side by side in a confined
glass booth (the staff treated us like visitors to

a maximum security ward) and sort through
Ann's as-yet-uncataloged papers (nobody
before us, in the ten years since they'd been
donated, had requested access). Or foreseen

what I would learn—her private life, when I
was her student, had such an air of mystery—
from a diary she kept in the mid-fifties. How
she felt torn between spending her total time

building up her daughters, or trying to live a
full adult life of her own. How she struggled
to write: interruptions every five minutes from
the children and telephone were death to any

continuous flow of thought—whole mornings
a vast horrible waste. How she wrestled with
self-doubt. How much rejection could she take?
Did her work have no value? Was it idiotic to

squander more time in such a competitive
unappreciative field? How both her parents
died within six months of each other: "and so
shall we, how this makes it clear to us, in our

turn." How disappointed she was when she
went to UCLA to hear Louise Bogan give
a talk, a talk she would not have missed for
anything because of her deep admiration for

her poetry and criticism. Ann noted Bogan's
resemblance to the "serene being" on her book
jackets: "small downward-darting upper lip,
the straight hair, parted in the middle above

an exceedingly high forehead—a tall woman
with a certain awkwardness or stiffness of
carriage and a seeming coldness." Her topic
being "the young poets," Ann hoped Bogan

might acknowledge someone she knew, even herself—although "this was a great thing to hope." When Bogan mentioned Barbara Gibbs, a mutual friend whom Bogan had helped get

a Guggenheim grant, Ann began to tremble in anticipation, but the talk ended there. Ann approached the platform, introduced herself. Miss Bogan seemed never to have heard of

Ann Stanford, though Ann had sent her a copy of her first book. "Oh," she lamented in her diary, "to be one of the names whom people, the important ones, recognize and wish to

talk with, to be one of this charmed, close literary world!" The way to accomplish this, she resolved, was through work, hard work. And how disappointed she was, finally, with

her own mentor, Yvor Winters, whom she'd studied with at Stanford University in the late thirties. Returning from Yosemite in September of 1956, she stopped to visit him

and his wife Janet Lewis, also a poet, at their home in Palo Alto. Ann was aware that his estimate of her work was not as high as when she was his student, but since she wanted to

apply for a Guggenheim, thought it best to go and see what he would give her in the way of a recommendation. She arrived in town early, so bided her time: ate crackers and cheese she

bought in a market, purchased a bathing cap
at a drugstore. Got slightly lost—slightly on
purpose? And still pulled up in front of the
Winters' house half an hour too soon. What

else could she do but fuss with her hair and
replace her lipstick long enough for Janet, who
must have been listening for her, to come out
to the car. Warm and friendly, same as always.

Unlike Winters, who, uncomfortable-looking
in suit and tie, bulkier than Ann remembered,
his face very red, as if his collar was choking
him, was clearly annoyed at having to waste

his afternoon in idle talk. Janet brought out
a tray of iced coffee and cookies. Ann did not
eat her whole cookie, as Winters' chilly gaze
from across the room killed her appetite. She

mentioned her plans to edit a book of poetry by
women. Winters, with a short laugh, scoffed,
"Ah, Ann, have you come to that?" Following
her husband's lead, Janet remarked that one

might as well have an anthology of blonde or
one-legged poets. (Ann would include Lewis
in *The Women Poets in English*, published in 1972.
Though the first collection of its kind, feminists,

perhaps because it seemed tame, shunned it.)
Winters sat puffing his curved pipe, silent for
long periods, contradicting when he did speak,
criticizing almost every poet Ann brought up,

"like a severe Dutch parent that one fears more
than understands or loves." When Ann asked
if he would recommend her for a Guggenheim,
Winters said he could praise her work "up to

a point." Ann did not ask to what point; she
left the Winters' house, surrounded by its grape
stake fence, determined never to burden him
again: "I shall seek him out no more." Yet she

did apply for the Guggenheim, and waited
each morning for the postman, thinking surely
he would bring word that she had received
a cherished fellowship. That news, of course,

never came. Instead she accepted her first
teaching job, at UCLA. The job might do
more for her, she reasoned, getting her out
into the world, than any fellowship would do.

What a bittersweet surprise to find, as I sat
with Maxine in that confined glass booth in
the Huntington Library, in the chaos of Ann's
uncataloged papers, the unfinished letter—

half typed, half handwritten—she'd begun
in support of my Guggenheim application:
"David Trinidad was a student of mine at
California Sate University, Northridge, in

the early seventies. Even in his early work,
he showed unusual talent. Over the years,
his writing has continued to develop in range
and precision, though his subject remains

most often the netherworld of the city with
its drug users, gay bars, and one-night stands."
As I read her words, my hands trembled. In
the bottom right corner of the page was my

old Los Angeles phone number. Just then,
Maxine came across May Swenson's letter,
the one that Rosanna had quoted from at
her mother's memorial. Half typed, half

handwritten—"Ann, my type ribbon ran
out. And no chance of getting another in this
backwoods place." (Ocean View, Delaware.)
The letter was dated more than a week after

Ann's death. And so we realized that Ann
never read her friend's last words to her. In
our glass booth, Maxine read them out loud:
"The beauty of your work is its clean simplicity,

of image, sound, message woven together
without artifice, to convey pure emotion
to the reader. Pure emotion is poetry's
task. It has become very rare among us."

I met May Swenson just once,

at the Dorland Mountain Colony
in Temecula, California, midway
between Los Angeles and San Diego,
in the week between Christmas
and New Year's, 1979.
I'd been selected as the first
writer-in-residence at the artists' retreat,
situated amidst 300 acres of hilly chaparral
homesteaded by Ellen Dorland, a world
famous concert pianist, and her
husband Robert in the 1930s.
Mrs. Dorland, widowed, in her nineties,
still lived on the premises, now
overseen by a nature conservancy.
Twenty-six years old, recuperating
from a serious automobile accident
(limping on one crutch), I had spent
a lonely six weeks, late October
to early December, in a rustic cabin
(I was the only resident; none
of the other cottages were finished
yet), trying to write poems, drinking
scotch into the night, waking
each day to the same desolate landscape—
sunlight burning the mist off
endless sagebrush. A dubious
honor, this fruitless residency:
I felt as if I had failed those
who'd bestowed their faith in me.
A few weeks after I returned home,
I was invited back to participate in a salon
with the second resident, May Swenson.

I didn't want to miss the opportunity
to meet her, so my sister drove me
down from L.A. for the day.
Everything about Swenson
screamed old-school literary lesbian:
butch Dutch Boy bangs, mannish
shirt and slacks, durable footwear.
Her weathered face seemed frozen
in a defiant book-jacket stare.
She had an unassailable air.
The salon was held in the main
house, Mrs. Dorland's, in a room
heavy with timeworn, out-of-place
objects: dark antique furniture,
framed photographs, silver
candlesticks, ornate jug-shaped
vases, bookcases with grilled doors,
brown-and-red rug on the floor.
Low-beamed ceiling. Cracked
adobe brick walls painted a dull yellow.
Mrs. Dorland sat at her Steinway
piano, white hair done up in
a Katharine Hepburn-esque bun,
and played something for us.
This was the fulfillment of her
and her dead husband's dream—
to provide a place for artists to
come together and share their work.
Zan Knudsen, May's companion, read
a chapter from a young-adult novel
about a misfit adolescent girl jock.
(Knudsen, I'd been told, was heir
to the dairy fortune; I don't know
how many times I'd bought
their pink container of low-fat

cottage cheese.) The colony's
first director, Elisabeth Des Marais,
a lovely woman with blonde hair
and milky skin, an aspiring playwright,
read from a piece in progress.
After I read my poem, everyone
turned to May. The seasoned
poet was expected to comment
(or pass judgment?) on the novice.
She said a few things; I only
remember that she didn't like
that I used the word "God"
in the last line. May did not
read a poem of her own. Her
contribution to the salon
was a tape of birds singing
that she'd made, with a cassette
recorder, on the Dorland grounds—
a bit too eccentric for my taste.
I'd brought a couple of her books
with me, but didn't ask her
to inscribe them. As much as
I admired her (in large part because
she was a good friend of Ann Stanford,
my college professor), it would
take me many years to fully
appreciate her quirky humor and
formal ingenuity, her fine mind.
At the end of my residency,
Elisabeth had had me sign
a plaque (she later burned my
signature into the wood) that
would hang in the cabin and
that subsequent residents would
also sign, so there would be

a personalized record of the artists
who had stayed there. May Swenson
signed her name right under mine.
Twenty-five years later, when
a wildfire swept through the
Dorland Mountain Colony,
destroying all ten of its buildings—
lost, Mrs. Dorland's 1920s Steinway,
her eclectic library, the treasures
she and Robert collected during
their travels—both of our names
were consumed by flames.

IV

Poets

After Ashbery

Alice Notley, Eileen Myles, Tim Dlugos, James
Schuyler, Joe Brainard, Tom Carey, Dennis Cooper,
Elaine Equi, Jerome Sala, Sharon Mesmer, Allen
Ginsberg, Joan Larkin, Mark Ameen, Susie Tim-
mons, Elio Schneeman, Paul Schmidt, John Ash-
bery, Douglas Crase, John Ash, Barbara Guest,
Kenward Elmslie, Ann Lauterbach, Anne Waldman,
Ron Padgett, David Shapiro, John Wieners, Gregory
Corso, Rene Ricard, Brad Gooch, Vincent Katz,
Michael Friedman, Ed Friedman, Robert Hershon,
Gerrit Henry, Douglas Oliver, Nicholas Christopher,
Honor Moore, Marjorie Welish, Bruce Andrews,
Charles North, John Tranter, William Corbett,
Alfred Corn, Marc Cohen, Andrei Codrescu, Amiri
Baraka, Kimberly Lyons, Harryette Mullen, Bob
Perelman, Lee Ann Brown, Jeffery Conway, Gillian
McCain, Lynn Crosbie, Chris Stroffolino, Maxine
Chernoff, Damon Krukowski, Peter Gizzi, Jaime
Manrique, Michael Lassell, Assotto Saint, Scott
Heim, Kenny Fries, Walta Borawski, Jim Cory, Karl
Tierney, Debra Weinstein, Gerry Gomez Pearlberg,
Dorothy Allison, Bea Gates, Sapphire, Sparrow,
Mike Topp, Tuli Kupferberg, Bob Flanagan, Amy
Gerstler, Kevin Killian, Dodie Bellamy, Robert
Glück, Susan Wheeler, David Lehman, Robert
Polito, Geoffrey O'Brien, Carl Phillips, Mary Karr,
Jessica Hagedorn, Dorianne Laux, Cornelius Eady,
Timothy Liu, Mark Bibbins, Kathleen Ossip, Shan-
na Compton, Soraya Shalforoosh, Edward Field,
Denise Duhamel, Mark Doty, Richard Howard,
Michael Klein, David Groff, Moira Egan, Molly
Peacock, Katy Lederer, Jean Valentine, Marilyn

Hacker, Robyn Selman, Lawrence Joseph, Jonathan
Galassi, Bob Holman, Prageeta Sharma, Patti Smith,
John Giorno, Lita Hornick, Vijay Seshadri, Sophie
Cabot Black, Jeanne Marie Beaumont, Anna Rabi-
nowitz, Adrienne Rich, Mary Oliver, Charles Simic,
James Tate, Jorie Graham, Lucy Grealy, Lucie
Brock-Broido, Robert Pinsky, Jason Shinder, Donna
Masini, Paul Muldoon, Donald Hall, Theodore
Weiss, Bernadette Mayer, Maureen Owen, Elinor
Nauen, Patricia Spears Jones, Paul Violi, Lewis
Warsh, Matthew Thorburn, George Green, Ed
Smith, Kim Rosenfield, Rob Fitterman, Martha
Rhodes, Peter Covino, Regie Cabico, Guillermo
Castro, Douglas A. Martin, David L. Ulin, J.D.
McClatchy, r. erica doyle, Robert Siek, Star Black,
Ethel Rackin, Hugh Seidman, Claudia Rankine,
Mark Levine, Connie Deanovich, Wayne Koes-
tenbaum, Bruce Hainley, Maggie Nelson, Cynthia
Zarin, Nathan Kernan, Richard Tayson, Mark
Wunderlich, Jana Harris, Stacy Doris, Joy Katz,
Vickie Karp, Charles Bernstein, Eve Packer, Laurie
Sheck, Shane D. Allison, Jenna Cardinale, Carly
Sachs, Wanda Coleman, Paul Hoover, Diane Wa-
koski, Maxine Scates, Carol Muske-Dukes, Lloyd
Schwartz, Frank Bidart, Jason Schneiderman,
Michael Broder, erica kaufman, Karen Weiser,
Anselm Berrigan, D.A. Powell, Rachel Zucker.

To Adrienne Rich

More than two decades have passed
since I interviewed you,
in New York for a big award ceremony
(you wouldn't win),
in a surprisingly austere
(where were the flowers?)
midtown hotel suite.

I worried if my borrowed
recorder was working
while you railed, impressively,
against the monstrous political machinery
that was diminishing
our human rights.

A photographer there
in the room with us
caught each impassioned
gesture.

Naive enough to be starstruck—
victim of the very commodification
you yourself condemned—
I hung on your every word.

At Ira's suggestion, I sent you
a single gardenia
afterwards, in gratitude.
And to spruce up that suite!
401, the same as our
West Broadway address—
a sign I took to be significant

when I'd nervously
arrived at the door.

Sarah Pettit helped me edit
the interview for *The Advocate*.
Sarah who would die young,
only two years later,
who once said Ira and I
were the most hedonistic
couple she knew.
We did eat and smoke
a lot, unapologetically
spent gobs of money.
How we reveled in the excesses
of the Clinton nineties—
the death throes of your
great patriarchal beast!

Later, I never forgave you,
Adrienne,
for your dismissiveness
when I asked you to endorse
Ann Stanford's poems,
help us rescue them
from obscurity.
You were honest
to the point of being unkind.
So much for sisterhood,
I thought. Your cause
the only worthy one.

Plath, in her journal,
sized you up:
"little, round & stumpy"
and "opinionated."

I secretly take some
satisfaction in that.

Yet I still have the books
I had you autograph—sentimental
to a fault. "In hope,"
you wrote in the one I open.
So grandiose! The poems
fail to draw me in. All
intelligence and fight, Adrienne,
but to my taste—

No, let Sylvia have the last word: "dull."

No More Blurbs

No more blurbs
No more letters of recommendation
No more MFA programs
No more low-residency degrees
No more chapbook competitions
No more first book prizes
No more Whiting Awards
No more Pushcart nominations
No more NEA grants
No more Guggenheim fellowships
No more MacArthur geniuses
No more Pulitzer winners
No more National Book Awards
No more NBCC finalists
No more Academy of American Poets
No more Poetry Society of America
No more *Best American Poetry*
No more poet-moms
No more prima donnas
No more self-promotion
No more judged by Mark Doty
No more selected by Louise Glück
No more chosen by John Ashbery
No "More of this sitting around like beasts!"
No more "There's only room for one at the top of the
    steeple."

Poets

At the dinner after his Dia
reading, A, whom I'd been
seated next to, turned to me
and said, "I read *Plasticville*.
It was strange." I didn't
ask him what he meant by
"strange." His comment
just hung there, in the uneasy
air between us. After I gave
a reading at Bennington
College, B, who taught there,
said, "That was strange."
I didn't ask him in what
way. In a Thai restaurant
in Chicago during AWP,
I told C, a Pulitzer winner,
what A and B had said.
"They're both academic
poets," he said, "and you're
not." He was coughing
and sneezing with a new
cold, which I kept mentally
protecting myself against.
At one point, he blew his
nose and a string of snot
caught on his salt-and-pepper
beard. I didn't tell him.
D told me that when she
went clothes shopping
with E, a Pulitzer winner,
E said to her, "If it fits, buy
six." And that when E

and F (her poet husband)
got divorced, F called E
a charlatan. That bothered
her—as would the outcries
of favoritism when Foetry
went after her. G told
me that at a poets' dinner
in New York, E refused
to acknowledge him: she
would only talk to the
other Pulitzer winners at
the table. H told me that
when she was E's student,
she would have killed for
her. I thought: "Killed?
Like a Manson chick?"
When my name came up
at a dinner party at which
Ira was present, J, a Pulitzer
winner (who obviously
didn't know Ira and I were
dating), said snidely, "Yes,
the *famous* David Trinidad."
It stung when Ira told me.
Why should J, who had
such power in the poetry
world, resent my tiny slice
of success. When I told
K, an FSG poet, what J had
said, he said, "After he's
dead, no one is going to
give a fuck about his work."
A story that went around:
L, a secondary Beat poet,
drunk at a downtown bar,

bragged that once M, Beat
poet supreme, died, he (L)
was gonna be Numero Uno.
Ira was incensed when N,
poet turned novelist, tried
to pitch his manuscript to
him at Cookie Mueller's
funeral. As was I when
I heard that O, without a
doubt the most successful
poet in America, said about
P, one of his closest friends
(and his better), "Yes, but
he didn't go to Harvard."
(Both O and P, for the record,
were Pulitzer winners.) A
well-known artist told me
(we were walking down
University Place after a book
party at Teachers & Writers)
that O had recently told him
all he wanted was to win
the Nobel Prize so he could
tell everyone to fuck off. I
thought: "But he already
does that." When I met Q,
who was reading with R
(his poet wife), he said, "I
thought your hair would be
different." That puzzled
me, but I didn't ask him to
explain. Someone (I forget
who) called R and Q "two
sharp operators." It was
rumored that Q "swung

both ways." Speaking of
coiffures, a fiction writer
in L.A. once said S, one of
the few women associated
with the Beat movement,
was "just a sweep of hair."
T (a great source of gossip)
told me that U, "the father
of confessional poetry," once
asked V (who would later
become New York State Poet
Laureate) if she wanted to
meet W, "the suicide poet."
V asked, "What's she like?"
U replied, "She's drunk and
egotistical, just like in her
poems." V said, "In that
case, no, I'll pass." "Life is
perpetually unfair," X told
me when I brought her to
read at Columbia College.
Her poetry was OK; the real
appeal was that she'd been
W's best friend. I took her
to the Art Institute where,
over lunch, she told me J was
one of her least favorite poets
(they'd read together at Dia).
When I asked her what she
thought of the proliferation
of poets in recent years, she
said, "I have a solution: each
one shoot one." She expressed
interest in my work (I wasn't
about to foist it on her), so I

sent her a copy of *Plasticville*,
from which she derived no
"intellectual pleasure." So
she said in an email: I had yet
to fully exploit my talent. At
a dinner during a Y (the other
"suicide poet") conference, I
was seated next to Z, who'd
come down with a cold I was
afraid of catching. She casually
turned to me and said, "Your
poems terrify me." "Why?" I
(at long last) asked. "Because
you just come out and say it."

(I need another alphabet.)

Susan takes me to the Academy of American Poets

reception for James Tate.
I can't imagine why
I agreed to go. Still some
hope of acceptance, I suppose.
I remember it as a series
of flashes, each more grim
than the last. Flash: the guest
of honor. "Nice to meet you,"
I say. "Nice to meet you,"
he echoes back. That's that.
To his right: John Ash. I smile
expecting recognition (we've
met on several occasions),
but he just glowers at me.
Looking past him, I see W.S.
Merwin (or rather his white
hair). I'm aware of Ashbery's
presence in the room, too. Flash:
Susan has me by the hand,
leading me through the crowd.
"I want you and Jorie to meet."
"*Susan.*" All eyes, it appears,
are upon us: sudden moves
make them nervous. I wait,
miserably, while Susan talks
to Graham. Finally: "Jorie,
this is David Trinidad." Susan
steps back; I trust her, so can't
fully grasp the extent of her
perversity. Graham regards
me fiercely. With heavily
mascaraed eyes. And haughty

toss of over-brushed, highlighted
hair. I manage a weak "hello."
She extends a limp, queenly
hand. Wrist heavily braceleted.
Fingers heavily ringed. It's
like shaking a dead—why traffic
in clichés. She takes Susan's
arm, turns her away from me,
introduces her to her former
brother-in-law. I retreat to
the outer edge of the crowd,
can't quite breathe. Everyone
eyeing, as they chat and sip
white wine from plastic glasses
and snatch hors d'oeuvres from
passing trays, everyone else.
Tensely entranced by such high
stakes. Bloodthirsty for the first
strike. It makes me feel sick.
What's Ron Padgett doing here?
This isn't his world—or is it?
Flash: Star Black (blonde, a bit
crazed) is in my face. "David
Trinidad! I know Eileen Myles!
I've read 'Meet The Supremes'!"
I'm never prepared for the pain
of hearing Eileen's name. She
gestures to a woman suddenly
at my side. "Have you met
Vickie Karp? Her cat just died."
I pray to God I said something
compassionate, didn't simply
stand there with my mouth
wide open. Flash: I've made
my way downstairs, to the

men's room, where I appraise
myself in the full-length mirror.
Black linen blazer all wrinkled,
barely hiding the sweat circles
under the arms of my (burnt
orange) shirt. My hair is getting
more and more gray. I need to
lose weight. Without telling
Susan, I wander outside, down
a colorless midtown street.
It's humid, about to storm. My
mother is dying in California.

Commonplace

So many lousy poets
So few good ones
What's the problem?
No innate love of
Words, no sense of
How the thing said
Is in the words, how
The words are themselves
The thing said

     —James Schuyler

*

I come finally to the conclusion that there are not many
really good writers.

     —William Carlos Williams (1947)

*

in the 19th century a bad poet was called a candle
waster.

     —Bernadette Mayer

*

As for fame I've had it
before I've
had it: meanwhile,
others grow vast on
very little

    —A.R. Ammons

  *

Everywhere in this city I see people writing poetry to
try to win prizes or notoriety. You can imagine what
they write. Anything I might say to them would no
doubt end in harsh words, so I pretend not to hear or
see them.

    —Bashō (1692)

  *

"His ruthless climb to the middle."

    —Tim Dlugos

  *

Friendship must be dependent on the way one's friend
lives up to one's own standards for friendship.

    —Ted Berrigan

  *

my friend the
    poet is no
longer attracted
to any
    center of which
he is not
the attraction

  —A.R. Ammons

*

It is one reason why I am content to leave New York
for good. Everybody is so intent on using everybody
else that there is no room or time for friendship any
more.

                —Elizabeth Bishop (1953)

*

      unless I find a place

apart from it, I am its slave

  —William Carlos Williams

V

Man with Toy

At forty-five,
what next, what next?
—Robert Lowell

The radiator is clanking

as if someone's hammering on
the pipes (time to get up) and Byron
is at the door, barking: he hears
Obie Benz climbing the stairs
to his office (the loft above us). Obie
made a documentary in the late eighties,
Heavy Petting—in which celebrities
like Allen Ginsberg, Sandra Bernhard,
Laurie Anderson, and William S. Burroughs
confessed their first sexual experiences—
that did quite well. *"Byron!"* We
never properly trained him, so such
pleas are pointless. Still, we yell
Shhh! Quiet! Shut the fuck up! Byron
looks at us, baffled for a second, then
goes right on barking. I finally
pull myself out of bed. Blessedly
I don't teach today. Ira sits at
the kitchen table, reading the *Times*.
I am no longer interested in the news.

From the left front window of our loft
(facing Spring Street), we can see
part of the Empire State Building—
a reminder, when I do notice it, how
lucky I am to live here. Lucky? Amazed
might be closer to the truth. Often,
walking down the street or hailing
a cab, I think: "You actually live here.
In New York City. Where you always,
since you read *Valley of the Dolls* as
a teenager, wanted to be." The glamour

instantly disappears when the next person
bumps me (intentionally?) without
saying "I'm sorry." Nothing makes
me angrier. Laura, my therapist, says
it requires constant negotiation:
too many people crowded into too
small a space. I try to imagine myself
old in Manhattan—walking a different
cairn terrier (Byron would be gone
by then), sitting alone in a brown booth
at the Knickerbocker—but can't.
This city is for the young or the rich.
I've never really liked it, would probably
have left after graduate school if I hadn't
met Ira. I tell myself (and others) that
the relationship is all that's keeping me here.

Everyone who is going to die has died—
for the time being, at any rate. Many
I once counted as friends are no longer
in my life. We still give dinner parties.
Who comes? Wayne Koestenbaum.
Susan and Philip. Robyn and Stacey.
Ira's publishing partner from London.
Gary. Betsy. Linda. Lynne. (More
Ira's friends than mine.) I see Elaine
on my own. And Jeffery. My therapist.
Is there no one else I can count on?
I've quit smoking—the hardest thing
I've ever done, harder than giving up
alcohol and drugs—and started collecting
toys from my childhood. Firmly
in my mid-forties, there's plenty of time
to waste. (Somehow I know this.)

When Ira launches his own agency,
he leases the loft below us and sets up
his offices there. Obie rarely works late,
so at night we have the building to
ourselves. I read how Elizabeth Taylor
and Richard Burton, at the height
of their stardom, booked the hotel rooms
above, below, and on either side
of theirs, to ensure privacy. I pretend
that Ira and I are the gay equivalent
of Irving Mansfield and Jacqueline
Susann, the *Sunday Times* (I do read
"Arts & Leisure") strewn all over
the green pin-striped duvet cover on
our queen-size bed (not enough room
for a king). Byron is our Josephine.

At the kitchen table, I write a long
skinny poem in Byron's voice—"*Every*
Night, Byron!"—a week in the life
of an urbane canine. Byron sits at my
feet whenever I work on it, as if he
knows what I'm up to. His vigil ends
as soon as I finish the poem. Ira objects
that I refer to us as "one for-the-most-
part-happy little alternative family."
"That's how Byron sees us," I say.
A lesbian couple, both named Debbie,
that we used to hang out with, once
told us they'd made a vow to always
stay together. In my heart (but not
my head?) I know Ira and I will not.

While Ira is in London on business
I read a book on the Zodiac Killer—
a garish yellow, red, and black true-crime
paperback—that keeps me awake: I
obsessively check the locks on the door
and the windows, the fire escape gate.
Must I, for the rest of my life, bar
windows and doors against the Manson
Family, the Zodiac, Richard Speck?
Byron would be no help: he'd probably
want an intruder to throw his pink
squeak-toy. Yet he'll wait at the door for
Obie's footsteps, run to the front windows
to bark at a motorcyclist revving his bike.

I sit at the middle window and watch
them film a scene from *Sex and the City*:
Sarah Jessica Parker and her redheaded
sidekick walking down West Broadway,
talking about their love lives, no doubt.
SoHo has been transformed (overnight,
it seems, though it must have been gradual)
from a relatively quiet neighborhood, that
came alive nights there were openings at
art galleries, into a teeming mecca of
high-end clothing stores. The sidewalks,
especially on weekends, thick with tourists
and shoppers, street vendors hawking
tacky T-shirts and third-rate paintings.
It's impossible to walk Byron, when it's
this crowded, without some kind of
altercation. I don't leave the apartment
all weekend, if I can help it, and suffer
when Ira isn't around to take Byron out.
Nights, too, are noisier: every brute

from Jersey, Long Island, and the other
boroughs comes into Manhattan to let
loose. On St. Patrick's Day, the Empire
State a lit emerald encased in mist, revelers
yell, smash glass, and get into fistfights.

The big reading at St. Mark's Church for
the Norton anthology of postmodern
poetry approaches. I dread being in
the same room as Eileen. The morning
of, I decide to burn all her letters to me.
Why should I cherish them when she
clearly has no regard for my friendship.
Destroying them will free, secretly
empower me, I think. Ira eggs me on.
I fill the kitchen sink with years of
correspondence: letters and postcards
with her sloppy handwriting and scrawl
of a signature (which I used to treasure),
photographs, manuscripts, poems I asked
her to write out by hand, the downward
squiggle on the blue cover of *Sappho's Boat*
that she drew for me and signed (which
I always meant to have framed). I light
the match. Ira fans the smoke toward
the open window. How I loved receiving
word from her, first in my studio in
Hollywood, then, after I got sober, my
studio in Silver Lake. When she stayed
with me at the latter, she ruined my yellow
teakettle while I was at work: turned on
the burner underneath it then forgot, went
out to the courtyard to sunbathe. I didn't
care about the teakettle at the time, but
ten years later, analyzing our friendship

with Laura, I did care that she didn't
apologize or offer to replace it. Once,
I sent her a magazine with two of my
new poems; "Tim's Stolen Sweater" was
one of them. She wrote back: "the best
of David." That had meant so much to me.
Now as I feed the letter to the flames, her
messy black handwriting crumples to ash.

I wake with a start from an afternoon nap.
Byron curled at my feet. I'd dozed off
while reading *Seth Speaks*—just a few
pages of his "you create your own reality"
channelings make my head heavy. Byron
growls, jumps off the bed, runs barking
to the door as Obie Benz descends the
stairs. I don't know (or care?) where Ira
is. It's beginning to get dark. As I fall
back asleep, Byron's barking fades. This
is how I am creating my middle age.

My Yoko Ono Moment

for Nick Twemlow

It's annoying
how much
junk mail
comes through
the slot
& accumulates
at the foot
of the stairs

mostly menus
from restaurants
in the neighborhood

endlessly
coming through
the slot

despite the sign
we put on the door:
No Advertisements
No Solicitors

One night
I scoop up the whole pile
on my way out
(as I do periodically)
& dump it
in the trash can
on the corner
of West Broadway & Spring

just as Yoko Ono
happens to be strolling
through SoHo
with a male companion

She watches me
toss the menus

then turns to her friend
& says, "I guess
no one reads those."

For Jeffery,

a poem in the offhand style
of Jimmy's post-Pulitzer period
to wish you happy birthday
(your fiftieth) and say
thank you
for twenty-five years of friendship.
Have we really been friends
that long, and for half
of your life?
I can't believe so many years—
a quarter of a century—
have passed since
I saw you, a handsome
young man (of twenty-five!)
standing at
the back of the bookstore
in West Hollywood where
I gave my last reading
as a resident of Los Angeles
before moving to the East Coast.
Years later we'd joke
you were my Eve: lurking
in the shadowy alley
outside the stage door
in her smudged trench coat,
stalking her prey:
the incomparable Margo—
aging and vulnerable, an imploding star.
We did end up living our own
version of *All About Eve*, didn't we:
two innocents from The Valley
bumbling our way

through a Lower East Side
poetry scene rife with Eves.
Slowly losing our idealism
(not to mention our tans).
The film only verified what we'd
learned from experience:
the "hurtful desire" for stardom
is the original sin.
Our flirtation, in those
suggestive letters we sent—
me in Brooklyn, you still in L.A.—
leapt straight to friendship
when you finally arrived in New York.
The romance just wasn't there, in person,
a deflation as easy to accept
as you were to trust.
How cinematic memories are:
scenes from a movie
that happens to
have been my life.
We plod up Second Avenue
one frigid night
after an A.A. meeting,
heads bent into the wind.
Your eyes watering from the cold.
Stubborn cigarette in my stiff
gloveless fingers.
(I believed, mistakenly, that
smoking would keep me warm.)
We sit, scarves wrapped
around our necks, at
the Ukrainian restaurant
and talk poetry and poets,
unable to reconcile
the admirable work

with the abominable behavior.
It's the late eighties
in the East Village
and Morrissey's plaintive voice
is everywhere.
By then, you'd been
evicted from two apartments
(due to nonpayment
and the antics
of your HIV-positive,
drug-addicted, Barbie-collecting
roommate Michael),
gotten sober,
and moved into
a room of your own
in the same SRO
on Third Street
where Quentin Crisp,
purple hair tucked
into his fabulous black hat,
was living out his
elderly years. Oh
to have been famous
when fame meant something.
The two of you waited
each day for the mail—
you for postcards
from a boyfriend
in Paris, Crisp
for letters from fans—
and sorted it together.
Your room, you told me,
was so small
it fit only a single bed
and side table

and shoe rack
on the back of the door,
which you filled
with espadrilles
of every color and stripe—
taupe, army green,
brown, black, yellow,
navy blue, red, white—
your final splurge,
via mail order, with James'
(your ex-lover in Los Angeles)
credit card. You never
wore them, just liked
to look at the colors.
"Every time I turn around
it's midnight," you
once said in grad school,
overwhelmed, as was I,
by the speed of New York life.
I met and moved in
with Ira. You met and
moved in with Ron.
The next time I turned
around, more than a decade had passed:
Ira and I had broken up,
9/11 had happened,
and I was about to move
to Chicago. We stand together
at the going-away party
Susan threw for me
in her Washington Square apartment,
ten floors up, at the window
of her south-facing dining room,
silently taking in the Towers' absence.
"It was the kind of

evening I always dreamed
of living, or walking into, like a movie,"
you would write in *Phoebe 2002*,
our 650-page collaborative epic
based on *All About Eve*.
"All those smart NY writers.
To honor a first-rate friend,
to say good-bye,
wish him luck,
and mean it,
even though I know
his absence will sear my heart."
The fruit balls, you noted,
were speared with picks
with paper pineapples
on the tips.
My parting gift
was to refer you to Laura,
my own therapist—
an Eve-like move up the ladder
after all! But you were in
crisis, it was the decent
thing to do.
And look how, more than
a decade later, you have come through.
So many memories, Jeffery.
But no time for more
if I'm ever going to finish this
offhanded poem. It's
already much longer
than I imagined it would be.
How did Jimmy
keep his so concise?
I must get to the mailbox
on the corner if it's to reach you

before your birthday.
I'd wanted to write about
the first Thanksgiving after
I broke up with Ira,
how you and Ron invited me
to your house in Woodstock,
how I walked along the towpath
alone, crying my heart out
to the white mist drifting
off the river through
the naked trees, not because
I'd broken up with Ira, but
because the shallow queens
who came to dinner
had promised to bring
a pumpkin pie and didn't,
and that was the one
and only thing I wanted.
But that's more about me than you.
Except that, out of kindness,
you made sure there was pumpkin pie
(and whipped cream) the next day.
Happy birthday, Jeffery.
I loved my fifties
(I'd escaped from New York!)
and hope you do too. And thank
you again for your friendship—
I don't know where I'd be
without it. Those suggestive letters
you wrote me, incidentally,
are with my papers
at NYU, for all the world to see.
I'm sorry.
If you still have the ones
I wrote you, please burn them.

I'm sure I sound an absolute fool.
When Rachel Zucker returned
from her trip to Schuyler's archive
in San Diego and told me
she'd read all my letters
to Jimmy, I was mortified.
"What were they like?"
I reluctantly asked. "Well,"
she replied,
"everyone's young once."

A Few Words About My Collecting

How many Barbie dolls will it take
To soothe your wounds? How many bubble cuts—
Brunette (your favorite), titian, platinum, ash blonde?
How many ponytails—blonde and brunette?

How many outfits—near mint, pristine, NRFB—
To take away the pain? How many accessories—
Sunglasses, gloves, necklaces, shoes, gold hoop
     earrings—
All so very hard to find? And so expensive—

The pale pink satin gown with long, draping train;
The delicate "Plantation Belle" dress, three tiers
Of frothy lace on tea-length skirt of dotted Swiss
     sheer—
You can barely bring yourself to handle them,

Though they're yours. (Well, not until you pay off
Your credit cards.) Being a poet in New York
Is too disappointing—it's all about politics, not
Good writing or camaraderie—it's too self-serving,

Too cutthroat—you don't want it anymore. Or
So you tell yourself. Oh, you still want it—admit it—
You're just not willing to pay the price, not willing
To turn yourself into a monster. (Or maybe you

Don't have what it takes.) What you do want
Is your childhood back—every last bit of it—
Every girlish toy you coveted but weren't allowed
To look at—let alone touch—plus everything

You did have that got tossed or lost long ago.
So you collect vintage Barbie—each doll, each outfit,
Each accessory—the way you used to hunt down
Out-of-print poetry books or smoke cigarettes or

Have sex—with the single-minded obsessiveness
Of the truly possessed. Already you have enough
To fill a small museum—not only with Barbie
But all your secondary collections: Liddle Kiddles

(You're particularly attached to Kiddle Kolognes
—Your sisters had them—thumb-sized dolls in
Plastic perfume bottles, each dressed as the flower
For which she's named—Rosebud, Apple Blossom,

Violet, Honeysuckle, Sweet Pea, Lily of the Valley—
Their artificial scent still redolent after thirty years),
Slickers (Yardley of London's mod lip gloss in
Those eye-catching—they drove you wild when

You were a teenager—orange-and-pink-striped tubes),
Petite Princess "fantasy furniture" (the blue satin
Chaise lounge—with the gold-trimmed bolster
    pillow—
Takes you back—Oh, to love miniatures is to kneel

Down like Alice and long for a world you're too big
To fit into), coloring books, boxes of Crayola crayons
(Preferably the 64-pack—with built-in sharpener—
How you love the litany of hues—Raw Umber,

Burnt Sienna, Aquamarine, Sea Green, Carnation
Pink, Magenta, Periwinkle, Thistle, Midnight Blue),

Disneykins (tiny Alice, miniscule Tinker Bell),
Paper dolls, troll dolls, *Classics Illustrated Junior* fairy
    tale

Comic books (Rapunzel letting down her ladder
Of long golden hair, the twelve princesses descending
A secret staircase to dance till dawn at an underground
Castle, Thumbelina floating downstream in half

A walnut shell), Plasticville buildings (HO scale),
Patty Duke and *Valley of the Dolls* memorabilia,
Board games, Colorforms, lunchboxes and
    thermoses—
And more. Dear forty-five-year-old self, I know

How desperately you want to find Lie Detector—
Mattel's 1960 "scientific crime game"—no batteries
Necessary to question twenty-four colorful suspects—
Which you—amateur detective—would do on
    summer

Afternoons—the Headwaiter's handlebar mustache,
The Night Club Singer's long cigarette holder,
The Gambler's tan complexion, the Actress' flashy
Clothes—savoring each clue. I know how much

You want Video Village, Milton Bradley's game
Based on the TV show you watched religiously
After school (contestants advanced on a life-sized
Playing board down three streets—Money Street,

Bridge Street, and Magic Mile—collecting cash
And prizes, losing turns, sliding in and out of jail
Through elastic bars, and fishing for wrapped gifts—
This thrilled you—from an arched step-bridge),

And how much you want Barbie's Fashion Shop
And Ideal's Haunted House and all sixteen volumes
Of *The Golden Book Encyclopedia* (your mother bought
A new one every week—at the local supermarket—

Until the set was complete—you'd spend hours
Poring over the color illustrations) and Aurora's
Plastic monster model kits (you had Dracula
And the Mummy, but always wanted the Bride

Of Frankenstein and—especially—the Witch) and
The April 24, 1964 issue of *Life*—with Richard Burton
As Hamlet on the cover—for the article on trolls—
The phenomenon of the fad—a girl in red leotard

And tights tethered to the ground—like Gulliver—
By an invading army of troll dolls—clouds of red,
Yellow, orange, and white hair sprouting from their
Impish heads (you'll locate the magazine soon

Enough—in a second-hand store in Florida—on
One of your last vacations with Ira). But locating
The precious object will only slake the ache
For a moment—before desire wakes—yet again—

And overtakes you. What if you obtain everything
You crave—what precipice will you face then?
A complete collection is a dead collection—or so
Says Susan Sontag. Oh tortured younger self—

I see you looking for answers in books—searching
For the cause of your conflicts and anxieties—
Your uneasiness with your own appetites. I see you
Sitting in therapy—week after week—struggling

To come to terms with your "hobby"—with cutthroat
Poets. Not until you read—years after you move
To Chicago—Emily Dickinson's "I had been hungry,
All the Years"—will you understand that it's better to

Be a person "outside Windows"—as the "Entering"
Only "takes away." Better to leave the playing field
To the monsters (since you don't have what it takes).
Better to refrain—and learn to cultivate—the ache—

What was I doing in Lawrence, Kansas,

in William Burroughs' lakefront cabin,
in the middle of a lightning storm—
multiple bolts flashing from
blue-black clouds,
illuminating the violet night sky,
jagged white laser beams randomly
pounding, it seemed, the ground,
sprouting veins, electrified tree-roots,
advancing across the helpless terrain
like an alien invasion.
Ira was on the phone with James:
Sure, we could go down to the basement,
but it might be locked, he didn't
know where the key was. No one
had been down there in years, god only
knew what we would find—spiders
and whatnot. We'd have to use
a flashlight. It was stuffed with old furniture.
From the kitchen window, I watched
the strikes get closer and closer
until, overcome with fear,
I crouched on the bathroom floor.
Thus passed the first night
of what was to be a two-week "vacation."
Every morning, I chauffeured Ira
(who didn't drive) around the lake
into town, to James' house, where
he and James would work all day on
Word Virus: The William S. Burroughs Reader,
then doubled back around the lake
to the cabin. I tried to read
and write, but went stir-crazy

meeting the gaze of the deer head
mounted above the stone fireplace.
So found myself roaming the area
in our rental car. I hit every used bookstore
and antique mall I could find.
In a display case of collectible toys,
I eyed Sheath Sensation, an early
Barbie outfit (fireman-red cotton sheath
with four gold buttons and two
deep pockets, short white gloves and
open-toe pumps, crisp straw hat with red
ribbon hatband), NRFB, and bought it
for $225.00. Not a bad price,
though it would make Ira mad.
This purchase, as far as I was concerned,
made the trip to Kansas worthwhile.
I bought a red felt Disneyland
pennant (pristine) for $10.00.
And a number of vintage DC comics,
which I read late at night after Ira
had fallen asleep: Superboy
and the Legion of Super-Heroes
in their colorful, tight-fitting costumes.
Each possessed his own unique power:
Chameleon Boy, Lightning Lad,
Sun Boy, Invisible Kid. It was mid-July,
and hot, so every day I found myself,
after shopping, at the stadium
movie theater on Iowa Street.
Twelve films to choose from. I saw,
in those two weeks, *Men in Black*,
Contact (twice), *The Fifth Element*,
Hercules, *Breakdown*, *Nothing to Lose*,
Love! Valour! Compassion!, *Operation Condor*,
Con Air, *Face/Off*, *A Simple Wish*,

and *My Best Friend's Wedding*.
I wanted to see *George of the Jungle*
because I thought Brendan Fraser
was cute, but never got around to it.
Each evening, we convened at
Burroughs' house for dinner.
Dragonflies flitted above the tall grass
in front of the famous bungalow—
painted barn-red with white trim.
A trellis on the side of the porch
dense with red rose blooms.
The screen door creaked open.
Bone-thin and frail, hunched forward,
Burroughs looked at me
suspiciously. I don't believe
anyone bothered to tell him
who I was. I had little interest
in his work. I'd read *Nova Express*
in college, only remembered
that I'd found it difficult. Did he sense
this? Or was it obvious—I didn't
fawn. He wore a green army jacket—
even in the heat—looked like he
was shrinking inside it. But not
from lack of sustenance. The literary
lion was well fed: salad with
Paul Newman's Ranch Dressing,
curried lamb, rice, snow peas, bread
and butter, strawberry shortcake.
We sat in a semicircle around him,
holding our plates, while he talked
nonstop throughout the meal,
in that growly gangster drawl
I was familiar with from his Nike ad.
I don't remember a word he said.

Periodically he began to choke
on his food, James futilely
reminding him not to talk
while chewing, and everyone froze.
Dear God, I thought, don't let
him drop dead in front of us.
(He would, in fact, die of a heart attack
two weeks after Ira and I went back
to New York.) Rather than sit
there uncomfortably, I helped clear
and wash the dishes. To me, the house
felt dark, oppressive. His collection
of hand-carved canes and walking sticks,
in an umbrella stand in the corner,
struck me as creepy—a far cry,
admittedly, from mass-produced
toys. Two red skull candles
on a ledge—one of them unlit,
the other burned halfway down.
I noticed, on the coffee table in
the dim living room, a burgundy-colored
paperback, Tennyson's *Selected Poems*.
I asked him about it. There were
great titles in there, he said, to be lifted.
He showed me "Ulysses"; I sat and
reread it in his presence. When
I took my notebook out to jot
something down (not about him),
they all (even Ira) pounced on me:
What are you writing? Note-taking
was verboten—who knew. If I
hadn't been chastised, I might not
have secretly taken the few notes I did.
That he liked gumdrops. That he
smoked pot throughout the evening.

That feeding the goldfish in the pond
in the backyard was the high point
of his day. At dusk one night,
two boys from Alabama knocked
on the screen door. One of them blond,
the other redheaded. Both utterly
in awe. He went out onto the porch
and talked with them, posed for
photographs with them, signed
books for them. On the sly, I recorded,
on a pink Post-it, my impressions
of him: energetic, fragile, childlike,
lonely/sad, wounded in some
fundamental and tragic way, sharp
and manipulative, didn't miss a thing.
On another Post-it, what James told
Ira to tell me to get at the market:
vodka (Smirnoff), rice, lima beans,
peaches 'n' cream ice cream.
Dennis Cooper's name came up
in conversation. "He'll get nothing
more from me," snapped Burroughs.
(Dennis had trashed him, apparently,
in print.) Toward the end of our
trip, he invited Ira and me to go
shooting with him. We declined.
Neither of us wanted anything to do
with guns. He produced a photograph
someone had taken of him through
the trellis, surrounded by red
roses. "A venerable old fuck
giving orders to his assassins
through the roses," he growled.
"Message of roses . . . message of roses."
I locked the bathroom door

behind me, pulled a pink Post-it
out of my back pocket,
and, like a spy, wrote it down—
just because I'd been told not to.

From a Notebook

NYC skyline
faintly aglimmer

through the darkened windows
of this car

4:49 a.m.
on the way

to LaGuardia

so many friends

dead

the second half
of my life

ahead

9/25/98

The Breakup Poem

It is stunning, it is a moment like no other,
when one's lover comes in and says I do not love you anymore.
                                                                —Anne Carson

Ira chose to drop the bomb
in the middle of a session
with Judy, our couples therapist:
I don't want to be in a relationship with you anymore.
"Really? You mean that?"
Yes. I'm done with it. I want out.
It came as a complete surprise. I thought
things had been getting better:
my collecting seemed to have run its course
and I was willing to start contributing
toward a country house,
which Ira insisted
he wanted, though I was the one
who would have to do all the driving.
Judy thought things had been getting better, too.
(I had to prod her to admit it.)
Ira and I had dinner plans
after our session, which we cut short,
with lesbian friends.
You mean you're not coming?
He said this incredulously.
"You're kidding, right?"
I left Judy's office in a daze
and took a cab back to our loft
and sat on the couch. Byron,
uncharacteristically, did not come out
from under the bed to greet me. I thought—
hoped, rather—that Ira would change his mind
and I'd hear the front door slam

and him bound up the stairs.
But no, he went out to dinner
with the lesbians. I sat there
as the room grew dim. In the stillness of dusk.
I thought, "This must be what it's like
to be told you're going to die:
you have to leave this life."
Goodbye Keith Haring refrigerator magnets:
orange radiant baby, blue angel,
green barking dog.
Goodbye three Nan Goldin photographs,
one of a young, sad-eyed Japanese man
and his collection of vintage Barbie dolls.
Goodbye cabinet full of flower-splashed Vera napkins
and tablecloths, picked up at antique malls
and flea markets.
Goodbye pair of Tiffany glass candlesticks.
Goodbye Eames coatrack with multi-colored balls.
Goodbye small Tom Slaughter painting—
a New York cityscape in primary colors—
that I convinced Ira to bid on
at a charity auction. He only
paid $250.00. No way
was he going to let me have it
in the "divorce settlement."
Goodbye painting.
Goodbye big red tulips flopping
all over the white oval Saarinen coffee table,
flat waxy petals open wide.
Goodbye.

I thought, in that moment, of an incident
that had occurred a few months earlier.
Driving to Woodstock.
The three of us in a rental car:

me nerve-wracked at the wheel;
Ira harping at me from the passenger seat;
Byron, frightened by our arguing,
cowering in the back.
I was relating yet another
disappointment in the poetry world
when Ira snapped, "Get over it, will you!"
He always fought against what I was feeling.
An inconvenience he felt obliged
but unable to fix. And impatience:
he never understood why I
couldn't grow a thicker skin.
How many times had I said to him,
in our sessions with Judy, "Just let me
have my feelings. They will pass."
I hate you, I spat.
We drove in silence
the rest of the way,
both stung by my declaration.
Byron, wagging his tail again,
excitedly took in the scenery.
Sitting in the dark apartment
saying goodbye to the things we had accumulated,
to the space we had shared for ten years,
I wondered if what I'd uttered was true.

When I told Helen, my "medical intuitive"
(L.A.-speak for "psychic"), about the breakup,
she said, "You should get down on your knees
and thank the powers that be
that he ended it. You would have
stayed with him out of loyalty.
Now you're free to develop
other aspects of yourself."
How could I have faith in the new unseen life

she said I was going to create.
Wayne Koestenbaum said, "Think
of the great breakup poems you'll get to write."
But I didn't wish to write such poems.
I respected Ira, had learned a lot from him
despite our differences—
or perhaps because of them.
I wouldn't want to write
anything that might hurt him.
Ira would continue to see
Judy individually.
For a while I was bitter
that they still had each other
after the failure of our joint therapy.
Two years later, 9/11
would force me to face
my resentment. Judy's husband,
Brian, was on the 104th floor
of the north tower. She found herself,
in that moment, a widow
with two young daughters.
Ira told me the news.
How could I comprehend the enormity of her loss.
I meant, in the numb months that followed
the horror, to communicate my compassion.
Only after I'd left New York
and was settled in Chicago
was I able to send her
an inadequate sympathy card.

Man with Toy

This miniature plastic tea set
survived unopened
for half a century
so he could find it
on the Internet
and purchase it
via PayPal
for $13.95.
Barbie-sized
but not Mattel
("Don't accept imitations!")
the age-spotted
label reads
"Made in Hong Kong"—
for one of Barbie's
wannabes
perhaps, that
not as expensively dressed clone,
ponytail of molded plastic,
that hung on toy racks
in five-and-dimes
in that bygone
era known as
the Sixties.
He loosens two
tarnished staples
and removes,
from the age-tinged
plastic bag, a blue
serving tray,
pink teapot (with lid),
pink pitcher,

four blue teacups and saucers
and slender "silver" spoons,
and arranges them
among similar
treasures
in the plexiglass
display case
on a bookshelf next to his desk—
each piece bright
and cheerful as
the day it was
manufactured,
in an exotic land halfway
around the world
from the suburb
where he coveted it
(or one like it)
as a boy, a trinket
untouched by fifty years
of wars and disasters,
a ten-cent toy
that traveled through
time and space
by virtue of its irrelevance
and mass-produced grace:

"Someone might want this one day."

VI

9/11

Does it really matter,
whether we photograph the disaster?
—Susan Rich

9/11

After we broke up, Ira kept the loft
on the third floor and I took the one
on the second, where his offices had been
(he'd moved them a while back, a few
blocks west, to the tenth floor of 180 Varick,
then disbanded his agency when he
became editor-in-chief at Grove/Atlantic).
Suddenly I was living like a college student
again—mattress, lamp, desk from IKEA.
Since I would have had to bicker with Ira
to get some of the things we'd bought
together, I exited the relationship "clean,"
with just *my* stuff: poetry books, collectibles,
art. Isermann starburst clock. *Password*
(silhouette cigarette spies) and *What Comes
Around Goes Around* (Liz Taylor wielding
gun) paintings. Pinkish Joe Brainard
(boy in shower). George Schneeman
(stockings on wire hanger with gem by
Alice Notley: "So may / I say that I
had a vision / last night of Heaven?").
Hung them on pale green walls. Missed,
most of all, watching movies, so had
a 27-inch Sony Trinitron delivered from
Circuit City in Union Square. DVDs
were new; I became obsessed with seeing
movies in their true aspect ratio. I was
aware, time to time, of Ira's movements
above me, on the high white tin tile ceiling.
More light than I was used to (it woke
me too early) and considerably more
noise, one floor lower, overlooking the

intersection of West Broadway and Spring.
I hated being closer to the push and
shove of SoHo, the madding crowd
moving, rapaciously, from shop to shop.
When the red tour buses turned onto
Spring, the heads of the sightseers sitting
up top would glide, like cardboard cutouts,
by my windows. Byron ran up and down
the stairs between apartments; Ira and I
called this "joint custody." Twice a week
I took the Trenton Local to New Brunswick
to teach at Rutgers, and every Tuesday
night taught a graduate poetry workshop
at The New School. Sold, bit by bit, on
eBay, the bulk of my Barbie collection
to supplement my adjunct income.
Almost immediately, Ira started dating
a nineteen-year-old Dutch boy named
Marc. I was surprised that it didn't bother
me. Yes, Ira had initiated the breakup,
and I was unsure of the future, but I'd
quickly accepted that I would be better off
single or with a more appropriate partner.
It bothered Marc, though, that Ira's ex
was living in the same building; it became
a point of contention between them. At
8:46 a.m. on the eleventh, I was sitting
in bed, in my underwear, working on
a poem. I heard the plane go overhead
and knew that something was wrong:
it was flying too low and too fast, and
made a whistling sound, like a missile.
Then a crash, as if two cars had collided
in the distance. And people shouting.
I pulled on my jeans and, barefoot, went

downstairs. From the front steps I could see
the towers straight down West Broadway.
It looked like a small plane had flown into
the one on the right. A taxi was stopped
in the middle of the street; the driver stood
beside it, staring up. I don't remember
smoke, just a hole, black, toward the top.
I could tell, from the sky surrounding
the towers, that it was a beautiful blue
day. The air felt mild. Ira appeared in
the doorway behind me. "I hope no one
is up there," I said. What did I know
about the World Trade Center, or what
went on there. I was in Manhattan to be
an artist. I noticed the towers sometimes
at night, walking home a bit weary after
teaching; or full after a late meal at Café
Loup; or after an event at the Poetry Project,
disenchanted with being in the thick of it.
Pretty, lit in alternating stripes—some
floors white, some black—but somewhat
abstract—it never consciously registered
that people were inside. I'd been up there
once, eleven years earlier, when my mother
and sisters and niece and nephew came
to New York for my graduation from
Brooklyn College. I found it the most
unnatural feeling in the world. My fear
of heights kicked in with a vengeance: legs
rubbery, stomach clenched; I felt as if
I were about to be plunged into the abyss.
While Ira and my family took photographs
of each other, I waited anxiously to return
to the elevator and ride down to solid
concrete and safety. "Oh, I think people

are," said Ira. He was going to vote, then
to his office. "Must you go?" Did I actually
say this? If I didn't, I certainly thought it.
I watched him walk down West Broadway
and turn left on Broome. I watched a man
set up a telescope on a tripod in the street
in front of our steps. By now, black smoke
was pouring out of the hole, into the blue
sky, and rising into the floors above it. Marc
had come down, saw what was happening,
and went back upstairs to get his camera.
I stood in the doorway, tentatively, half
in and half out of the building, holding
the door open, while Marc ventured down
into the street to film the burning tower.
Traffic had all but ceased. Sirens, far-off
sounding, west and south of us, wailed
toward that desperate height—surely they
would be able to help. People passed
on the sidewalk and in the street. Some
walked quickly, without glancing back;
others paused, turned, and froze in place.
"Oh! Oh!" I looked up to see a burst of flames
in the middle of the second tower. My
only thought was that the fire in the first
tower must have caused an explosion in
the second. "It was an airplane," exclaimed
Marc, leaping up on the steps. "I didn't
see it," I said. "Do you want to?" He had
caught it on his camera, held it up to me:
the two towers tiny in the flip-out screen.
I told him no. (He would ask me again
later in the day, and again I'd tell him no.)
More and more people were streaming
from lower Manhattan—most stunned

and silent. Noticed one woman crying.
And a man on a cell phone, gesturing
wildly. "They just hit the Pentagon!" he
yelled as he went by. I looked up: were
planes going to keep falling out of the sky?
When the man with the telescope said "I
can see people jumping," I went inside.
Byron was up in Ira's apartment; in the
stairway, I debated whether to bring him
down to mine. He was safe there, I decided,
asleep under the bed (I hoped), oblivious
to the chaos. I entered my place and turned
the television on: there were the stricken
towers, smoke billowing from both, and
that clear blue sky. A male newscaster
was saying, "This is going to change us
forever." On another channel: a slow-
motion replay of the airplane heading
toward the south side of the second tower—
what I couldn't see from where I stood
on the steps. On yet another: the flames
I had seen, papers raining down, screams
from a crowd witnessing the impact off-
screen. I turned down the sound and
called my father in California, to let him
know I was OK. An early riser, he was
watching it on his TV. "All I can say,"
he said, "is it's a good thing your mother
isn't alive to see this." I hung up and
called Susan. She could see the towers
from the dining room window of her
tenth-floor apartment on Washington
Square. She had to get ready, she said,
to teach. It wasn't lost on me that the two
people I'd felt closest to in the nineties

both reacted as if this was business as usual. I knew enough to stay right where I was, and be scared. I looked out the window: the intersection was filled with people, all staring downtown. I called Ira at his office. "This is serious," I said, "You should be here." The moment I hung up, a terrible, collective wail came from the crowd outside. I turned around to see, on the soundless TV, the second tower collapse under an avalanche of plunging, gray-white clouds. A half hour later: the same terrible wail from outside, the same terrible spectacle on my silent TV. I have no memory of what I did in the interval. The next time I peered out the window, the crowd was gone: nothing left to look at except smoke and an unexpectedly vacant sky. On the television, thousands were passing into Brooklyn on the bridge, behind them an ominous, expanding brown cloud. I pointed the remote at it, brought up the sound. Felt a bit safer to hear the newscaster say that Manhattan had been closed to traffic, and to hear, at last, Ira's footsteps above my head. In the afternoon, when he and I took Byron out, the streets were virtually empty. We walked to the market on the corner of Thompson and Prince, M & O, so I could stock up; we didn't know how long the city would be cut off. Ira waited outside the store with Byron. I filled my handbasket—with what? cans of tuna?

Progresso soup?—then got in line, a long
one that wound around the counter and
halfway down an aisle. As I inched
toward the front, I glanced back at the
other people in line: all were stiff and quiet
and scared—I could see it in their eyes.
The woman directly behind me—thin,
middle-aged, Italian—kept bumping me.
Normally that would have set me off,
but not today. She was nervous—I got
that. "Just get me out of here," I thought.
At the register, after I'd emptied my
basket and the cashier was finally ringing
me up, the woman pushed her items
forward, poking me, hard, at the same
time. The cashier began to ring up
her stuff. "Those aren't mine," I said
flatly, "they're hers." The cashier (she
was wearing a white smock) looked up;
I saw fear in her eyes. Confusion as
we tried to separate the woman's items
from mine. The woman—still pushing—
acted huffy, as if this was my fault. "If
you weren't so pushy," I snapped, "your
things wouldn't have gotten mixed up
with mine." Surprise at first, then her
face hardened with indignation: "I guess
everyone's ugly today." My comeback
was involuntary: "Shut your stupid mouth."
The cashier looked freaked out. Would
this escalate into violence? bloodshed?
death? I left the store shaking, helpless
with anger, overcome with self-reproach:
why couldn't I keep *my* mouth shut. Ira
had never had much sympathy for my

post-altercation regrets: he would have
told the woman off and thought nothing
more about it. Back at our building, Byron
came in with me. After it got dark, Ira
knocked on the door. He and Marc were
going to the supermarket at LaGuardia
and Bleecker, did I want to come with?
I did; I could stock up more. On the way,
a celebrity sighting: Harrison Ford. Surreal
to see Indiana Jones in a business suit,
on the day that was going to change us
forever, strolling down Prince Street with
two other men, also in suits, smiling and
relaxed—perhaps they'd just enjoyed
a good meal. In the market, the bread
aisle was bare, except for one loaf of
potato bread on a bottom shelf. This
brought to mind how, during the Cuban
Missile Crisis, supermarket shelves were
stripped clean. Nine years old at the time,
I didn't understand how adults could be
so frightened they would panic into mob
behavior, or how grocery stores could run
out of food. For days, the air was sepia
colored. Someone (I don't recall who) said,
"We're breathing people." The smell—
Jeffery remembers it as "chemically" or
"plasticy"—lingered for at least a week.
The wind would shift and you'd be reminded
it was still here. Everyone south of Canal
Street had been ordered to evacuate; we
were two blocks north, so were safe. Or
got to stay, I should say. I watched, out my
window, countless people drag suitcases
up West Broadway, hunched forward like

refugees, white surgical masks over their
mouths and noses. Houston Street was
cordoned off; every time I left SoHo,
I had to show my ID to a policeman
when I wanted to go home, to prove that I
belonged there. I remember thinking this is
probably the only time I'll get to see who
really lives in Manhattan. The first time
I took the subway (to Penn Station, to take
the Trenton Local to Rutgers), I sat across
from a young woman. We were the only
two in the subway car. We looked at
one another, but didn't speak. In all the
tight spaces—the trains, the greengrocers,
the streets—New York was a different place:
people were actually being nice to each
other. Maybe it was true—we had been
changed. Then Bush, worried about the
sagging economy, came on TV and said
that, as an act of patriotism, Americans
should go out and spend money. The day
after Thanksgiving, Black Friday, the crowds
came back. And soon after: street vendors
and sightseers, those mammoth red tour
buses stalled in traffic. I kept the green
curtains drawn. SoHo was once more
a hub of thriving commerce, and looked
like a trampled amusement park by the
end of each day: a place people came to
to push and shove from shop to shop,
and drop their trash. The usual ugliness.

VII

Two Odes

Ode to Frank O'Hara

It was your New York I wanted,
but I came twenty years too late.
Careerism had, by the eighties,
taken hold of bohemia.
Naively, I walked the streets
of a Manhattan that didn't exist.
Found out the hard way
and mourned, longed for,
as Bill Corbett wrote in 2001,
"the downtown scene where poets,
painters, musicians and dancers
worked and played together
as, alas, they seldom do today."

In the fourteen years I lived there,
whenever I passed 90 University Place,
your home from 1957 to 1959,
I touched the door. Fleetingly.
For luck. And simply to say hello.
Then, it was painted green.

The week after the attacks
on the World Trade Center, I took
my New School workshop
on an O'Hara walking tour. Fliers
of the missing had been put up
everywhere—covering walls,
phone booths, subway entrances, lampposts—
haunting emblems of dwindling hope.
Maybe a loved one was lying unconscious
in a hospital bed, or wandering
the streets with amnesia.

No one wanted to say
what, by now, we knew.

It was a misty night. Clear
plastic sheets were draped
over the faces of the missing—
to protect them. Beads of moisture
ran down the plastic, across
the fogged-up, ghostly tableaus.

A dozen of us stood, conspicuous
in the mist, in front of your address.
We were all in shock. (I don't know how
we made it through that semester.)
One by one, my students stepped forward
and touched the green door.

I also showed them the Cedar Tavern
on the corner, where you hobnobbed
with your artist friends
in the crush of the smoke-filled bar,
though that wasn't where it was located,
I studiously pointed out, in your time.

Jenna Cardinale and Shane D. Allison
were in that workshop. Who else?
I wrote to Jenna; she refreshed my memory:
Ben Bagocius, Theresa Collins,
Christine Scanlon, Anita Naegeli,
Carly Sachs, erica kaufman,
Ani Grigorian, Matthew Freedman
(or Freeman), Rachel Rear,
and Dave Gunton, who left,
Jenna says, after that semester.

In the spring, Shane, who I thought
had talent but was contemptuous
of any of our suggestions,
showed me, during one
of our conferences, a poem he said
an online magazine was planning to publish.
He wanted my permission.
A mash note addressed to me,
it contained the line: "I will deliver
truckloads of cum to your front door."
I told him I thought it was inappropriate
and asked him not to publish it.
He agreed, then went ahead
and published it anyway.
When I asked him to take it down,
he refused. I called Robert Polito,
my boss at The New School,
and explained the situation.
He didn't think it was a problem.
"Robert, if a male student
published something like that
about a female instructor,
wouldn't you think it was a problem?"
I resented having to explain it,
but it did the trick. Polito got Shane
to remove it from the Internet.

(Years later, Shane contacted me
in Chicago, and apologized.
I accepted his amends. Still,
he continues to mention
the incident in interviews—
"I wasn't too happy about
everything that went down"—
and recently published a poem

that says, "the poet David
Trinidad threatened to get me
kicked out of school." Which is,
for the record, far from the truth.)

The day before the New Year's Eve
before 9/11, I lay in my pale green
loft, under a two-shades-of-pink
and orange mohair throw,
and reread Alice Notley's *When I Was Alive*.
The radiators rattled. Byron crunched
his breakfast in front of the stove.
Shovels scraped the sidewalk
outside. I wrote a poem
about that moment—
"No Greater Pleasure"—
in which I liken the snow in the windows
to a shaken souvenir from my
first trip to Manhattan, almost twenty
years before: "that long-lost
swirling snowdome now home."

(As soon as I claimed New York
as home, ironically, it was time to go.)

I sent the poem to Alice.
She wrote back that she thought
that kind of good will between
poets was a thing of the past.

So be it.

Although I wasn't permitted to go
inside, at least I got to touch the door.

At Sexton's Grave

August 17, 2002

A story. (Let it come.)

Thirteen days before I moved to Chicago,
I flew to Boston to spend the weekend
with Damon Krukowski and Naomi Yang
(professionally known as Damon & Naomi).
Of all of Ira's and my friends, I
liked them the most. Gentle, intelligent,
talented souls. Having been burned
by the music business, they were determined to
create on their own terms. We'd spent time together
on Fire Island, in Paris, in Las Vegas (where
Ira and I were witnesses at their wedding), in our
respective cities. We trekked to Portland, Maine,
in the dead of winter, in search of secondhand
    treasures.
Rode scooters on Nantucket one summer.
When we drove to New Hampshire
to visit the Simics, I had an attack of hay fever.
(My one chance to socialize with Charlie
and I couldn't stop sneezing or blowing my nose.)
I have a photograph of Naomi and me
in the Angie Dickinson Room
(lined with framed glamour shots of the actress)
at Mary's, a restaurant in the West Village.
She's hoisting an obscene piece
of heavily frosted coconut cake
(from Magnolia Bakery) to my mouth—
it must be my birthday, one in my mid-forties.
I'm wearing a bright green shirt
with white stripes. The cake,

that snowbank of sweetness,
isn't going to do my waistline any good.

Damon and Naomi had always
wanted to introduce me to the poets Lloyd Schwartz
and Frank Bidart. (Lloyd's boyfriend David
and Frank both lived in the building next to theirs.)
At last, on the verge of my leaving New York,
we were able to make it happen.

Friday morning, Naomi picked me
up at Logan Airport and drove
us to Cambridge. It was extremely hot—
high 90s—and humid. After I
greeted Damon and settled in, we sat and chatted
for a while. Then the three of us, sweating profusely,
went to the all-poetry Grolier Book Shop
in Harvard Square. For many years,
the Grolier had been my favorite
place on planet earth. Nothing but poetry
to peruse—shelf after promising shelf.
Damon and Naomi left me, briefly,
to say hello to Beck, who was having
a tech rehearsal at Sanders Theatre
on the other side of Harvard Yard.
I stayed in the air-conditioned bookstore
and continued browsing. And struck up
a conversation with Louisa Solano,
the Grolier's legendary proprietor.
I had to ask: "Did you know Anne Sexton?
Did she come here to shop?" The answer
was no, but Louisa told me she'd attended
Anne's last reading at Harvard. "She was a mess:
drunk and on drugs. She slurred her
words, wandered all over the stage.

The audience was whistling and shouting,
'Anne! Anne! We love you, Anne!'
Egging her on. They wanted her to act
outlandishly. It was very sad."

Dinner that evening was magical:
a five-hour talkfest with Frank and Lloyd
in Damon and Naomi's garden.
Candles, those fairy lights, twinkling
all about. The smell of incense
(to ward off mosquitoes) pungently pleasant.
Fountain burbling in the background like a
    soundtrack.
Bottle after bottle of Pellegrino.
The food amazing: olive tapenade, radishes
dipped in salt, melon and prosciutto,
grilled salmon and polenta, fresh blueberries
with the most delicious yogurt/whipped cream
    topping.
And the company wonderful.
Frank and Lloyd both lovers of film,
so we had a lot to discuss. (Frank,
Naomi told me, owned so many DVDs
they were piled throughout his apartment
like a hoarder's newspapers.) When Fellini
came up, Damon said he was fond of *Roma*;
Naomi reminded us of the ecclesiastic fashion show
toward the end: nuns in black silk habits,
with gigantic white cornets flapping like wings
(à la Sister Bertrille); priests whizzing
past on bicycles and roller skates;
bishops sashaying down the catwalk, vestments
like huge lace doilies or paper snowflakes
over their red cassocks, swinging smoking brass
    censers

as if they were chichi handbags on chains;
even skeletons parading gossamer shrouds.
We gabbed about dozens
of movies, as Pellegrino and cappuccino
were being poured, but *Roma* is the only one
I noted when I wrote about that night
for *Phoebe 2002*.

I had to ask: "Did either of you
know Anne Sexton?"
Frank said he'd met her socially a couple of times,
that she wasn't the diva he expected.
She became obsessed, added Lloyd, with Elizabeth
    Bishop
when Bishop was teaching at Harvard
in the seventies, would leave
little gifts at her office door.

Then came the ceremonious
signing of books. (I'd picked up one by each
of them earlier that day, at the Grolier.)
"For David," wrote Frank in *Desire*,
"wonderful poet—I envy constantly when I read you
the cheeky candor, panache, poise, eloquence,
bravado of your work." And
if that wasn't flattering enough: "from a fan."
In *Cairo Traffic*, Lloyd wrote: "At last—
a much anticipated meeting. And a pleasure.
With thanks for your wonderful,
indispensible poems."
They both handed me a copy
of *Plasticville*. I froze.
A kind of shyness? stage fright? refusal to effuse?
My inscriptions were self-conscious, stiff.

Saturday morning after breakfast,
Naomi asked me if I would like to visit
Anne Sexton's grave.
She remembered that I'd wanted to do this
on a previous trip. "Can we?"
Damon did a search on Findagrave.com
and we were off in their white Saab.
Stopped at a deli for drinks, I stared at some
sunflowers—$1.00 each—but it didn't
register till we were back on the road:
I should have bought one to bring to Anne!
In tribute to her poem "The Sun" or the end
of "Live": "the sun, / the dream, the excitable gift."
We started looking for a florist—
I thought maybe I'd buy some daisies, Anne's favorite.
Naomi spotted a sign—FRESH FLOWERS—
and we found ourselves in a strange establishment:
a thrift store with a refrigerated glass case
full of wilting blooms. I put together
a decent bouquet (lavender and white spider mums),
which the shopkeeper wrapped in cellophane
then tied with a peach ribbon.

Thinking that I would find her,
thinking I would commune
with her spirit, we drove south
to Jamaica Plain, passed through
Forest Hills' gothic arch,
and consulted the cemetery map.
Anne is buried in the SS section (I couldn't help
but think of Sexton's bad Plath-inspired Nazi tropes).
e.e. cummings is also buried at Forest Hills,
in section E ("*Capital* 'E,'" Naomi observed).
We followed Greenwood to Hillside,
parked near Ardisia Path. As Naomi removed

the cellophane from the flowers, Damon and I
walked up a slope in search of Anne. Out of nowhere,
an eagle swooped in front of us, flew over
some headstones, landed high in an oak.
Damon and I were stunned . . . it seemed like such a
    sign.
We wandered about looking for Anne's grave,
but couldn't find it. I began to doubt that we would.

Suddenly I saw it: SEXTON. "Here it is!"
The family plot, a few feet from
where the eagle had flown in front of us,
and where it still perched, almost directly overhead,
as if guarding Anne's grave.

(At home, I would look up
the bird's "magical meaning"
on the Internet: *Capable of reaching zenith,*
great perception, bridging worlds.
When the Roman emperor Augustus died in A.D. 14,
his body was carried to the Campus Martius.
There a towering pyramidal funeral pyre
had been built, and the emperor was placed upon it.
As the torch was applied to the base
of the pyre, men in the surrounding crowd
cast their adornments into the flames. The fire
crept upward and an eagle was released
from the summit of the burning mound,
symbolizing the ascent of Augustus' soul to the gods.
Welsh legend told of how the souls of brave warriors
flew to heaven in the form of eagles.
In ancient Sumer, the eagle brought the new souls
of children to this world and carried departed souls
to the underworld. In Syria, the eagle

carried souls to its master, the sun.
The Hopi believed the dead rose to become
clouds drifting in an eagle-ruled sky.
They also kept captive golden eagles, believing them
to be messengers that could take their prayers
to the spirits.)

"She probably stood where we're standing
when she was alive." Naomi's words
gave me chills. Other fans who had made pilgrimages
had left pens for her. Pens! A cup full of them
on her tombstone. Some
had left photographs, letters.
Silently, self-consciously, I formed a prayer
(to be delivered on golden wings?)
as stiff as my inscriptions the night before,
thanking her for her poems, rich
with the imprint of experience,
carried with me all the years
(*The Complete Poems*, bought
at Papa Bach Books in West Los Angeles
in 1981, her name embossed in silver
on the black hardback, my treasured bible)
and instrumental in the journey
it took to reach this precise moment—
the verge of leaving New York
and venturing into the unknown, the next adventure.
Thus, on a humid afternoon in August of 2002,
at Sexton's grave, I whispered
God bless you, Anne.
I rested the spider mums, tied
with a peach bow, underneath her name, her dates.
Naomi took a picture of me, half in shadow,
leaning against the trunk of the umbrella pine

close to the grave:
straight lips, black sunglasses, hair going gray.
We got back in the white Saab and drove away.

Even so, this story ends with me still standing
where she once stood, breathless with blind faith.

VIII

Leaving New York

Leaving New York

I was leaving New York with a certain sadness and with profound admiration . . . it had given me the most useful experience of my life. I must thank it for many things . . .
—Lorca

The day I left New York
it was pouring rain like
the end of *Breakfast at Tiffany's*
(the movie). Fitting—
my idea of the city
had never been realistic.
I said goodbye to Ira and Byron
in the downstairs loft.
Byron had seen my suitcase,
knew I was leaving. It
took me by surprise,
seeing him so upset,
and woke me to the reality
of the moment. I
started to cry. "Are we
making a mistake?"
Ira had asked this two
or three times since we'd
broken up, and here
it was again—at the last
minute. He was crouched
down, holding onto
Byron, who was trying
to squirm free. I was
worried about getting
a taxi in the rain.
"No, this is for the best."
He looked up at me.

"I felt taken advantage of."
"That was never my intention,"
I replied. Still crying,
I hailed a cab, sat drenched
in the back seat as it
pulled away, rain pounding
the roof, streaking down
the windows. Right
turn on Houston. I
was off—almost. A few
blocks east, at Lafayette,
we hit a big puddle;
the engine died. When
the driver couldn't
get it started, I tried to
hand him some bills
through the partition.
He refused: his fault,
he insisted. I let them fall
into the front anyway,
got out, flagged down
another taxi, and made it
to JFK with time to spare.
It appeared New York
wanted me to leave
as much as I wanted
to leave it. At the gate,
I called Ira on my cell
phone (my first) and burst
into tears all over again:
*I'm sorry. Thank you for
our life together. I love you.
Goodbye.* Still crying
as my Xanax took effect
during takeoff, as the plane

rose above the storm
and I floated in blue
toward the future.

Of course New York
kept calling me back—
for readings, to research
Tim's, then my, life.
(I'd sold my papers—
thirty years of letters,
worksheets, notebooks,
even photographs—
to NYU before moving.)
It's a strangeness like
none other: revisiting
your own past in the
hush of the Fales Library
reading room. My
first trip back, after a
massage with Jeffery's
therapist, I walked
down Seventh Avenue
in a blissed-out daze,
and it came to me that I
should thank the city
for all the opportunities
it had given me, for
all it had taught me.
So I did. I talked to it.
And prayed for Jimmy
as I passed St. Vincent's,
where I visited him
the day before he died.
That night, introducing
me at a reading at

the Bowery Poetry Club,
Karen Weiser said,
"New York misses you,
David." It felt as if
the city was talking
to me, too, through
her. A sadness like
none other: returning,
time and time again,
to the place that had
inflicted such confusion,
such pain, then leaving
(often after a magical,
whirlwind trip) in
a cab speeding up
FDR Drive, the East
River glittering in late
morning sunlight.
Only to arrive the next
time, at LaGuardia,
wait for your suitcase
(with the black leather
Eiffel Tower tag) at
the carousel, wait
in the taxi queue, then
drive in silence toward
the Midtown Tunnel.
Skyline comes into view
—no Twin Towers—
and the cemetery (I never
did learn its name)
directly underneath it—
the eye following all
those headstones
into the jagged line

of skyscrapers. In this
way, New York always
reminds you of your
irrelevance: death awaits
all this teeming of life.
Once on the island,
however, perspective
dissolves and you return
to the streets, prisoner of
your own self-importance.

The Washington Square
Hotel, close to where
I once lived, became my
new headquarters. I
loved that each room had two,
sometimes three framed
headshots of iconic movie
stars, with full-blown
lavender roses decaled on
the glass. You never
knew which stars you
were going to get. Clark
Gable and Norma Shearer?
Katharine Hepburn and
Jean Harlow? Joan Crawford,
Gary Cooper, and Myrna Loy?
In the cramped restaurant
downstairs: an omelette
in a booth below Klimt's
The Kiss—a kitschy tiled
reproduction. Outside:
trees in Washington Square
cloaked with snow, after
a fresh snowfall. In all

weathers, the perpetually
young NYU students,
the drug pushers, the
ancient lady walking her
terrier. It hobbles after,
wearing a little coat.

I didn't really leave
New York until ten years
after I moved. Elaine
brought me back to read
in the Poetry Forum at
The New School. The circle
was complete: a decade
later, a reading at
the school where I taught
for seven years, where
I learned to be a teacher.
And it was spring!
Introducing me, Elaine
said, "In the poems of
David Trinidad, the TV
is always on." Afterwards,
Mark Bibbins told me that
as I was reading, in the
window behind me, there
was a striking pink sunset.
My parting gift. The next
day, in a taxi on the way
to LaGuardia, I was at peace
with the skyline: beautiful
and still, beneath a clearing
sky (it had rained in the
night). "If I never come back

here again," I thought, "I
would be fine with that."

When all is said and done,
my most enduring memories of
New York have nothing to
do with people or poetry.
Just a few private instances.
Driving one morning at
5:00 a.m., late in the nineties,
in a car with darkened
windows, to the airport—
off to read somewhere
or visit family in California—
and seeing a purple sunrise
begin to break through
a bank of black clouds.
I was being driven into
a watercolor. And aware,
as the car clip-clopped across
the Williamsburg Bridge, that
half my life was behind me.
(Definitely a glass-half-empty
feeling.) Walking down
Sixth Avenue carrying a green
and white Balducci's bag
(the only time I ever
felt like a New Yorker).
Bunches of parti-colored
tulips outside a greengrocer.
A glimpse, at dusk, of pink
at the end of street. Still
relatively new to New York,
getting caught in a downpour

without an umbrella near
Tompkins Square Park. I
stood in a doorway and
smoked a cigarette, waited
for the deluge to pass. Or
desultory in the back of a cab
watching Fifth Avenue,
deserted on Sunday morning,
whiz by (on my way to meet
Jeannie to go to a doll show
in Hackensack), but perking
up when I saw the facade
of Tiffany & Co. and, the
wistful strains of "Moon
River" stirring in my
dispirited mind, pictured
Audrey Hepburn sipping
coffee and munching
a croissant as she gazes
into the store, comforted by
(and here I quote from
the book, not the movie)
"the quietness and
the proud look of it;
nothing very bad could
happen to you there."

Byron wants his belly rubbed

so I do
& think of
all he's seen
me go through:

> several books
> Barbie
> quitting smoking
> my mother's death
>
> the depressed years in SoHo
> "divorce"
> 9/11
> escape from New York

& how he
came to
join me
in Chicago:

> When Ira & Bob Morris
> were newly dating, Byron took
> a nip at Bob's pants leg
> as he was leaving a dinner party
> at Ira's loft. Bob told the story
> in his column in the Styles section
> of the Sunday *New York Times*.
> "He doesn't like it when people
> leave," Ira said in Byron's defense.
> This Bob's uneasiness did not appease:
> "When it was time to retire, I
> would hear a growl and feel

a lunge from under the bed."
So Ira, who had insisted, when
we separated, that Byron was *his*
property, carted him off
"to a quiet neighborhood
in the Midwest" (i.e., my
apartment in Andersonville).
Byron's a less neurotic dog now,
Bob concluded. & so he is:
prancing down semisuburban
West Hollywood Avenue
with its green grass & trees
(which he happily pees upon)
instead of gray West Broadway
with its "mountainous turds
of black-bagged garbage"
(as Jimmy would say) &
early-morning procession
of earthquaking trash trucks.
I like to think Byron knew
his mischievous little nips
would warrant him a ticket west.

Not bad:
Byron had
made it into
the *Times*.

"Nice ink,"
as Ira would say.
But not his
first time

in print
by any means.

Aside from
my poems,

he's appeared
in a couple
of books.
The first was

> when Ira had a falling-out
> with his childhood friend
> Eric, who . . . let's just say Eric
> had airs. In revenge, Eric
> wrote a thinly veiled memoir
> of his strained relationship with Ira
> & the summer the three of us
> shared a house on Fire Island.
> (Ira & I spent a total of seven
> summers in Cherry Grove.)
> The names were changed to
> protect . . . someone. Ira became
> "Matthew." I, the generic
> "boyfriend." Byron, "Charles":
> "as in *Prince*" (though it's not as if
> we went around calling Byron
> *Lord*). With Eric, all was "divine,"
> "glorious," "pristine," "exquisite."
> He uses his memoir to even
> the score over a lost game of
> Scrabble. Ira had challenged
> one of Eric's words: *azures.*
> "There's no plural of *azure.*"
> Eric was out 69 points (triple
> word score). Injustice: "I felt
> strongly that the beauty of my
> word had been seriously tarnished

by this erroneous attack." But
the piece commemorates, ultimately,
the end of a longtime friendship.
What Eric went through with Ira
("I had lost my trust for him")
reminds me of what I experienced
with Eileen—will that ever *not* hurt?
I couldn't see it at the time,
but Eric nails Ira's character:
"cynical," "abrupt," "even rude":
"Matthew, more than anyone,
embodied the ideal of true
New York manic pace." I can
admit this now that I, too,
am free of Ira, establishing a new
life for myself here in Chicago.
Eric's memoir, which he published
in the Dutton anthology *Friends
and Lovers: Gay Men Write About
the Families They Create*, ends
with "Matthew" & the narrator
sitting together on a bench
in Washington Square Park
watching the princely "Charles"
rollick in the dog run: "There
we were, the two of us, in black
jeans and motorcycle jackets,
one barely looking at the other,
the breath of our words visible
in the clear, heavy, cold night."

Heartening
to be able
to appreciate
as moving

something that,
out of loyalty to Ira,
I once mocked.
The trustworthy

generic "boyfriend."
Byron jumps
up on the red couch,
curls at my feet.

Comforting.
Which brings us to
his second
literary cameo:

> When Lynn Crosbie visited us
> on Fire Island, end of August
> 1995, she was (by her own
> admission) a complete mess.
> She wrote about it at the beginning
> of her book *Paul's Case*. Obsessed
> with Paul Bernardo, the serial killer
> & rapist (who would be sentenced
> in Canada that September first),
> & full of fear, Lynn watched
> Ira & I dive "into the surf
> with bright red boards." She
> followed us in & was knocked
> over by a wave. "When I tried
> to stand up I was pulled under
> and thrown into another wave.
> I ran, choking and falling, to
> the shore, and wouldn't go back."
> Later I sat with Lynn ("crumpled
> miserably") in the beach house

& read her Anne Sexton's poem
"Imitations of Drowning," written
in 1962 when the strangler was
terrorizing Boston: "There
is no news in fear / but in the end
it's fear / that drowns you."
Then we played Scrabble (without
incident) & listened (on repeat)
to "Happy Heart," the upbeat
1969 Andy Williams hit. At
sunset, we took Byron for a walk
on the beach. As is his wont,
he barked at each dead horseshoe
crab we encountered. He seized
one shell & shook it: a swarm of baby
crabs fell out. Lynn was appalled.
The sky burned orange-red.
We'd made arrangements for her
to stay in our landlord's study—
designed like a ship captain's quarters—
separate from our rental. Unable
to sleep, she stared up at a school
assignment tacked to the wall.
For a creative writing course.
"Write a List Poem," it said.
She grimly complied: claustrophobe
cabin, scattering crabs, vampiric
mosquito bites, serial killers
peering through pitch-black portholes.
Overcome with fear, Lynn jumped
ship: ran back into the main
house & turned on all the lights.
In the morning, she told me
that when Byron heard her knocking
about, he came out of our bedroom

to comfort her: licked her face,
stuck close to her on the couch
until daybreak chased the murderers
away. She was so touched
by this, it led to her decision
to adopt a canine of her own.

Never one to
pass up the
opportunity to
pen a list poem:

What Byron Barks At

squirrels
deer
horseshoe crab shells
revving motorcycles

thunder
skateboards
balloons
UPS men

Which
brings
us
to:

When Ira's office was on the tenth
floor of 180 Varick, one of the
publishers he shared the space with
was Andrea Juno, co-founder
of RE/Search, the press responsible
for such titles as *The Atrocity Exhibition*,

Incredibly Strange Films, & *Angry
Women*. Their *Modern Primitives*
played a big part in the popularity
of piercing & tattooing, scarification.
The cover alone made me queasy:
a hooded, naked, heavily tattooed
man? woman? with a python
wrapped around his/her chest.
(At least the background was
deep pink.) New to New York
(she'd moved from San Francisco),
Andrea (or AJ, as she was called)
complained she was sitting home alone
night after night. So we invited
her to a few dinner parties at our loft.
I can no longer conjure her
face (& there are no pictures
of her online), only shoulder-length
straight hair—but what color?
Dark red, if I had to guess . . . dyed.
She seemed to suffer from a
persecution complex. "I don't
know why everyone is against
me," she whined, "I'm a *nice*
person." "Nice" isn't exactly
how I would have described her,
but I just smiled & offered
her more dessert. Once a week
I walked over to Varick to
write checks (Ira preferred
to keep the business "in the family"
—like a Mafia don) & would
usually bring Byron with me.
He'd run around & greet
everyone, then, when he realized

they weren't there to play with
him, go to sleep under my desk.
One day, after he'd barked
at a black UPS man who'd
startled him awake, AJ came
up to me & said, "I think
your dog is a racist." I should
have shot back, "I think *you're* a racist
for saying such a thing." But
just smiled & cut another check.
I knew Byron barked at all
UPS men, regardless of color.
When Ira's relationship with his
British business partner soured
& he decided to dissolve his
company to accept a position as
editor-in-chief of Grove/Atlantic,
AJ & the other publisher in
the Varick space turned against
him. I was with Ira his last
night there. Just the two of us;
everyone else had left. The last check
had been written, the last box
taped & labeled. I looked
around at the bare desks &
empty bookcases. Looked out
the window at the sweeping view
of lower Manhattan: all lit up
but, given the circumstance,
anything but inspiring. As we
were walking to the elevator,
Ira sidestepped into AJ's office.
I followed. It was dark & quiet
& spooky, trespassing on someone
else's personal space. Was

Ira going to take something?
Vandalize her office in some way?
No, he was going to mark it.
To my utter surprise (&, I
must admit, titillation), he
unzipped his fly and pissed
on the potted ficus in the corner.

After fourteen
years in the
asphalt jungle,
Andersonville,

with its flowers
& birds & blue sky,
feels like a living
cartoon.

"Time for a walk."
Byron leaps
off the couch
as I

reach for
his leash,
excited
to be going

outside.

Almost twenty years later, Eileen and I met

for lunch in Los Angeles.
She was living there at the time.
I'd come to town to read
from my new book, *The Late Show*,
at the Hammer Museum.
We agreed, via email, to meet
in the restaurant
at the top of the Angeleno,
the circular hotel where
the Hammer had put me up.
Eileen was late. While I waited,
I watched the traffic zoom by
below, on the San Diego Freeway.
Sick-looking palm trees
in the Brentwood hills.
Monolithic high-rises in the distance.
All shrouded in a familiar brown haze.
Strange to be merely a visitor
in a place that used to be home.
When she finally arrived,
I studied her face: deep lines
around the eyes, bags
sagging underneath them
like melting wax,
long cracks
down both sides, framed
by loose unwashed strands of gray.
It was a ruined face,
the face she deserved, I felt,
that she had earned.
As we talked, between bites

of Caesar salad and sips
of Diet Coke, I realized
it was impossible to have
a substantive conversation with her.
She's poison,
I told myself. *You must remember that.*
I did and didn't remember.
Three years later, when she
came through Chicago to promote
her new book, *Inferno*, I accepted
her lunch invitation.
She'd moved back
to New York by then.
Elaine had told me Eileen
was in a "nice phase"—
she'd won a prestigious award,
had a new young girlfriend.
We met at Tamarind
in the South Loop.
I arrived first, sat against
the green bamboo wall,
an orange pillow between
the wood bench and my back.
Nothing had changed,
except she was feeling magnanimous
because she'd won
a prestigious award and
had a new girlfriend,
thirty-six years her junior,
whom she'd met at the funeral
of Charles Bernstein's daughter.
When the high of the award
wore off and the girlfriend
eventually left her, how "nice"

would Eileen still be?
Over a California roll
and Diet Coke (with lime),
she told me that at the dinner
for Jimmy following his Dia reading,
when she went to sit
down next to him, Barbara Guest
said, "What's *she* doing sitting
next to him? She's the help."
(Eileen had been Jimmy's assistant.)
How everyone heard,
and how humiliated she felt.
Ironic: it hurt that Jimmy
hadn't thought to invite me
to that dinner, and that others
had noticed my absence
and commented on it.
Thinking about it in retrospect,
I wondered which had hurt more.
Eileen also told me she'd
recently, in a restaurant
in New York, been seated
at a table next to Ira.
He pretended not to know her.
She wasn't about to let
him get away with that.
"Hello," she said. "Hello,"
he said, disdainfully.
"Ira never liked you, Eileen."
At last I'd said it.
She winced.
You have to keep remembering
she's poison.
Part of a past life.

At the end of our meal,
she gave me a signed copy
of her book (which I sold
without reading) and a cookie
she'd gotten on her flight.
I didn't eat it.

After Ginsberg

I
What have I left out?

That Dennis once told me he and Tim had seen Eileen
    kicking a parked car in the East Village. What was
    she angry about? Who mad at? This before I
    moved to New York. An unheeded warning?

That Duncan Hannah once saw Greta Garbo buying a
    pair of men's pajamas. What else could he do but
    stop and stare.

That when Duncan was talking with Joe Brainard
    about the fact that Joe was going to die relatively
    soon, Joe looked at him and said, "At least I won't
    have to go to any more poetry readings." Then
    after a beat: "You will, though."

That after shopping at St. Mark's Books, Joe handed
    Elaine the new Ashbery (*Hotel Lautréamont*) he'd
    just bought. "Here, you take it," he said. "John can
    be so difficult."

That Joe once told Tom Carey about a breakdown
    Jimmy had while staying with Joe and Kenward in
    Maine. "That must have been difficult," said Tom.
    "It wasn't so bad for me," said Joe, "I got to be one
    of the disciples. Kenward, though, was Judas."

That Brad Gooch once described, at a dinner party at
    Nathan's, what it was like to work for Joe in the
    early seventies. Joe on speed, his loft floor covered

with images for collages. Joe would ask Brad to find everything red: flowers, jewels, Lucky Strike bull's-eye, five of diamonds, torn ticket stub. Then to find all the parakeets, all the butterflies, all the musical notes, etc. Brad said he didn't last very long.

Guest checks with pink heart in puff of cigarette smoke and pink rose commemorative stamp (35¢) at end of painted-in stem. Blue stage curtains, Pegasus, night sky with stars. Tab Hunter surrounded by pansies. Faceless boy in white underwear, spread-eagle on bed . . .

II
What have I forgotten?

A group of us—Ira and I, Nan Goldin, Amy Scholder, Eric Latzky, Dale Peck—at a restaurant in Little Italy. Nan, at head of the table, lifts her camera to snap a picture. I raise my hand to stop her. She seems taken aback—this probably doesn't happen very often. Everyone else turns toward me. If looks could kill, I would've looked like Faye Dunaway at the end of *Bonnie and Clyde*. I'd ruined their chance to be in a Nan Goldin photograph. But it bothered me that she hadn't asked.

How many pasta dinners at Karen Rinaldi's West Village apartment (where Waverly meets Gay). Donald Antrim, Rick Moody, Jeffrey Eugenides, Heather Lewis (who would later commit suicide), dear Lisa Teasley (whom I would huddle with at end of long table). No horror stories, just big ego fiction banter. Karen, who worked in publishing, gave me my boxed, three-volume, silver-and-black set of Proust.

Standing alone with Lucy Grealy after poetry reading at The New School. By a window. The challenge of making chitchat while looking into her disfigured face. Later she would die of a heroin overdose. But that day she was wearing a summer dress.

My fury when Robyn Selman introduced me to Lucie Brock-Broido: "This is David Trinidad. He collects Barbie dolls." Lucie was gracious. Later hopelessly trying to explain to Robyn why this demeaned me.

That at the aforementioned dinner party at Nathan's, Eileen brought up class (she always does). In this case, an anecdote about feeling slighted by Lucie Brock-Broido.

That at the end of April 1990, when Kevin Killian and Dennis Cooper, who both idolized Schuyler, happened to be in Manhattan at the same time, I organized a small dinner at Café La Strada in the East Village so they could meet Jimmy. There were baskets of bread and white flowers on the pushed-together tables. The younger writers talked among themselves; they were too shy, too intimidated to talk to Jimmy. Only Ira, who was socially fearless, related to him. Dennis took Polaroid portraits of everyone: Ira and Jimmy; James McCourt and Tom Carey; Mark Ewert and Dodie Bellamy; "bon vivant" Kevin Killian; Eileen and me. Eileen, in white sweat- over blue work-shirt, is gesturing adamantly; I (in black) glare back. Blurred white

blooms and lemon slice (on edge of glass) in fore-
ground. The only photograph I have of the two of
us. (I destroyed all the rest.) Underneath it, she
signed my name and I signed hers.

That there exist no pictures of me and Jimmy. No
pictures of me and Tim.

That at the Jimmy dinner, Eileen admitted she was
jealous of my ability to bring friends together. "I
can't do that," she said. One week later, when she
read with Jimmy at St. Mark's, she organized a
dinner afterwards. And made a point of not invit-
ing me to it. Joan almost split herself in half with
guilt, as the reading was breaking up, because she'd
been invited and I hadn't. (Poured on the pity)

That on June 27, 1989, Eileen said, "Poems should burst
into the place where everything's flaming and
alive." I loved that so much I jotted it down.

That two days later, walking with Eileen on Third
Street, I spotted a box sticking out of a trash can
and exclaimed, "Look! A Barbie Beach Taxi!"
Eileen smirked and said, "Great. Now she can run
down a Ken O'Hara."

That once, sitting with Jimmy in nerve-wracking
silence in his narrow Chelsea digs, I took the
plunge and asked about Frank O'Hara. "How did
you meet him?" "Oh, it's a long story that will keep
for a winter's evening." Then back to silence.

That at rehearsal at Raymond's for big Dia reading,
Jimmy was almost moved to tears when he read

"To Frank O'Hara": "and now people you never met will meet / and talk about your work." When he told me afterwards how this rattled him, I encouraged him to read it anyway. He shook his head no. There would be none of that. (Pathos)

III

Where else but in poem put Tim Dlugos Social
   Security number: 230-76-5135.

Or that Tim once called Philip Monaghan from 21 to
   say "I'm having lunch at 21!"

Or message Jimmy left on my phone machine on
   September 2, 1989: "Well, my name is James
   Schuyler and I write poetry in my spare time.
   And, well, am I being a bore?"

Where else list movies (written in old datebooks) I
   saw with Jimmy between August 19, 1988 and
   November 23, 1990: *Midnight Run*, *Married to the
   Mob*, *Young Guns*, *Mr. North*, *Sweet Hearts Dance*,
   Punchline, *Women on the Verge of a Nervous Break-
   down*, *Tequila Sunrise*, *Working Girl*, *Dangerous
   Liaisons*, *True Believer*, *Out Cold*, *Jacknife*, *The
   Accused*, *Field of Dreams*, *Great Balls of Fire!*, *The
   Fabulous Baker Boys*, *Back to the Future Part II*, *Bad
   Influence*; *After Dark, My Sweet*; *L'Atalante*.

When Jimmy was obsessed with *Bull Durham* (and its
   star, Kevin Costner), he tried to convince Ashbery
   to see it. But Ashbery refused because Jimmy had
   not wanted to see *his* favorite movie, *Who Framed
   Roger Rabbit*. So neither saw each other's film.

Where else "set down for posterity" (as Tim would
say) their childish aesthetic standoff.

I sometimes wondered, riding the F train back to
Brooklyn after a visit with Jimmy, why I wasn't
writing down any of the things he said. Why I
wasn't keeping a journal of my encounters with
such illustrious writers. I suppose I would have felt
like a spy, writing about them on the sly. Standing,
in part, outside my life. I wanted to be in it—as
completely as possible. I somehow knew that if I
ever did write about my experiences in New York,
I would remember what I was supposed to remem-
ber. That what I needed would be there, for the
poems.

IV
Still angry at Morris Golde for yelling at me outside
Elephant & Castle on Greenwich Avenue (I was
leaving with a friend) when I told him, thinking
he'd be pleased, that Tim's papers had been placed
at NYU. "How much did you get?" "We donated
them." "What! Why didn't you sell them! You
could've gotten money!" I was just happy Tim's
poems weren't sitting in a closet at home anymore;
they were now someplace safe.

Bittersweet to discover, in 2012, an online auction of
Morris' personal effects. A decade after his death.
Morris' name not mentioned, but I recognized the
provenance by inscriptions in the books. Books his
illustrious friends had signed to him. Kenward
Elmslie, John Ashbery, Joe Brainard. Several of
Tim's. Sold to the highest bidder.

Still angry twenty-five years later at idiot who re-
viewed *Hand Over Heart* for some fag rag: "David
Trinidad is a pop-culture-obsessed little twit
without the slightest command of the English
language." Another small-minded queen trying to
make a name for himself in gay publishing. He
long forgotten—even dead? But not his stinging
words.

Still angry at Charlotte Sheedy, the agent who, as a
favor to Ira, took me on as a client. I had just
finished the manuscript of *Plasticville*. "Why aren't
you as famous as Mark Doty," she said when she
and Ira and I had a meal at a meaty French restau-
rant on Spring Street. As if that were somehow my
fault. (Maybe it was?) "You should do some radio,"
she said. "Get yourself on NPR." Slowly, she sent
my manuscript to all the big presses. And for-
warded me the rejections as they came in. The
worst from Harry Ford at Knopf: "Why are you
bothering me with this crap?" After that, I asked
her not to send any more. A year and a half
elapsed. At a boutique on Thompson Street, I
bought a red Dharma doll and filled in one of its
eyes. (I was to fill in the other eye, the shopkeeper
instructed, when my wish came true.) Not long
after, Charlotte summoned me to her office. I
thought perhaps she had good news. Her hand-
some young assistant sat in on our conversation.
(As witness, I later realized.) His aghast expression
as she gave me a good dressing-down. It was my
fault, she made it clear, not hers, that she had failed
to find a publisher for my book. (Maybe she was
right.) Thus washing her hands of the matter. I
rode the elevator down and, walking west on

Bleecker, wept. I was finally one of those people
you see occasionally in New York: adrift on the
street, defenses stripped, unable to conceal how
futile the city has made them feel.

V

I regret that I wasn't nicer to Lita Hornick when I met
her. At John Giorno dinner party at "The Bunker,"
222 Bowery, where Burroughs lived in the seven-
ties. Alice Notley and Lita sitting against a concrete
wall. Alice: "Lita, do you know David Trinidad?"
Lita: "Only from his poems." A hint of excitement,
at meeting me, in her voice. My cue—which I
shamefully blew. Stiffly I stood, appalled by what
Tim called, in his diary, her fascinating ugliness.
Massive frame. Babyish aged face. Huge pearls
around her drooping neck. White hair pulled,
tightly, into golf-ball topknot. Just after we sat
down to eat, Lita, saying she wasn't feeling well,
stood up and left. I've always felt responsible: if I'd
been pleasant, she might have stayed.

It's no excuse, but I was in such a wounded place.

If I could reshoot that scene, I'd bow down and thank
her for her service to poetry, gush how much I love
the books she published with her Kulchur Press.

As an amends, I included (seven years after she died)
some of her collaborations in an anthology I
edited. One with Ron Padgett, "White Mink," a
favorite.

Clothes are my weakness, poetry my strength
Because it covers my body's and my soul's length.

The first line obviously, charmingly hers.

"Does this," I asked Lita in spirit, "make up for my slight?"

Came her answer: *I am wearing my new white mink tonight*

Snow on the ground outside

and inside:
mauve mums
in the fluted red
vase I bought
at Marshall Field's
(later Macy's)
after I moved
to Chicago.
Mums so right
for winter light:
pinkish-white.
And so unlike
Jimmy's fiery
flowers. This
morning I'm
revisiting him
("write some
skinny poems")
remembering
the many times,
walking to or
from a movie
and dinner, we
had to pause
on 23rd Street
because of the
pain in his leg.
He'd stand for
a few minutes
in the middle of
the sidewalk,

dividing, like
a rock, the swift
current of pass-
ersby, until the
pain subsided
and he was able
to continue on.
Those were long
minutes (New
York never stands
still) awkward
as the silences
when we'd sit
in his room at
the Chelsea Hotel.
Reticent (or just
shut down?) and
I reverent, shy—
and there was so
much I wanted to
ask him! Neither
of us was as open
as our poems—
easy to see now.
Recently, reading
his art criticism,
I learned the term
intimism: a practice
among painters
of selecting as
subject matter
familiar or inti-
mate scenes or
occasions from

their everyday
life. This applies
to literature, too.
Nice that there's
a tradition for
what you do:
trudge home
from the super-
market in the
snow, holding
a bouquet of
mauve mums—
white flakes on
the cellophane.
My first Christ-
mas in New York,
I bought him a
round glass vase
(very '80s) at
Macy's—and got
stuck on the sub-
way on the way
back. For nearly
an hour, everyone
on the crowded
car sat, sometimes
in the dark, and
silently waited,
except one man
who occasionally
swore under
his breath. It
seemed incon-
ceivable that

Jimmy, who
freely spoke
the language
of flowers,
didn't own
a vase.

Poems in this book have appeared in *The Ampersand Review, Amsterdam Quarterly, Bloom, Columbia: A Journal of Literature and Art, Columbia Poetry Review, Court Green, The Dream Closet* (Secretary Press, 2015), *The Gay & Lesbian Review, glitterMOB, Kettle Blue Review, Ladowich, Phantom, Pinwheel, Poem-a-Day* (Academy of American Poets), *The Poetry Project Newsletter,* and *Women's Studies Quarterly.*

David Trinidad's other books include *Dear Prudence: New and Selected Poems* (2011) and *Peyton Place: A Haiku Soap Opera* (2013), both published by Turtle Point Press. He is also the editor of *A Fast Life: The Collected Poems of Tim Dlugos* (Nightboat Books, 2011). Trinidad lives in Chicago, where he is a Professor of Creative Writing/Poetry at Columbia College.

68048369R00144